THE
WHITE
SHAMAN

A NOVEL BY

⤝ C. W. NICOL ⤞

THE
WHITE
SHAMAN

McCLELLAND AND STEWART

FIRST EDITION

The Canadian Publishers
McClelland and Stewart Limited
25 Hollinger Road, Toronto M4B 3G2

Canadian Cataloguing in Publication Data

Nicol, Clive, 1940-
The white shaman
ISBN 0-7710-6767-4
I. Title.
PS8577.I382W58   C813'.5'4   C79-094334-4
PR9199.3.N532W58

Designed by *Janis Capone*

PRINTED AND BOUND IN CANADA

to truth
reason
and the child of both

⤙ AUTHOR'S NOTE ⤙

In Canada, in official documents, and gradually in daily usage, the word *Eskimo* is being replaced by the term used by the people themselves, *Inuit*. The word *Eskimo* has derogatory origins, and the Inuit do not generally like it. I have therefore used the word *Inuit*, except in places where reported conversations of the late 1950s appear. The Inuit words used in the novel are of Eastern Arctic dialects, which sometimes differ from area to area.

ahowlik — old-squaw duck
amautik — deep-hooded woman's parka or over-jacket
angakok — magician, shaman
anorak — over-jacket
igloo — snow-block house
ilitsitsok, also *ilisitsoq* — sorcerer, evil magician
Inuk — human, Eskimo
inukshuk — anthropomorphic rock formations, statues
Inuit (sing. or *pl.)* — "the people," or Eskimos
Inuktitut, also *Inuititut* — language of the Inuit

innua — the spirit or soul contained in natural things; the
  "spirit owner" of a thing
Kabluna (*sing.* or *pl*). — the white man
kamik — sealskin boots
kayak — *lit.* "man's boat," a single-holed Inuit canoe
komatik — long Eastern Arctic dogsled
kudlu — soapstone lamp
muktuk — skin of beluga, a delicacy
nanook — polar bear
sila — the soul essence, a force permeating all things
tadloak — hunting screen, used for camouflage
tapirisat — brotherhood
teamik — tea
toodlik — loon
tornait — spirit, sometimes malevolent
tupilak — demon created by a sorcerer
ulu — woman's knife

THE
WHITE
SHAMAN

SPECIAL

Richard Tavett, the young British explorer believed to have been drowned in a canoe accident in Hudson Bay in 1958, then reputedly sighted by Eskimos in the following year after an extensive air search, has turned up alive, but once again disappeared. According to first reports, the young man escaped from the RCMP early this morning after injuring one officer and an Eskimo special constable. It is believed that he was accidentally shot in his escape. No further news is available at this moment.

— the *Montreal Star*, October 1, 1960

"You know, we been hearing a lot of hot-headed talk today, lots of fancy words about revolution and self-government and stuff. Lots of fancy politic words. Lawyer words. Makes me think. It's like when the old people sit around the table and drink tea and cough and spit and talk about the way things used to be, and about how strong and straight and true we Inuit were in the old days. Most young folks tend to get impatient and turn away, go watch television, take a walk down to the beer hall, make endless nothing-talk on the telephone. I always used to get real frustrated, because the old people used words I don't know, and if you asked them, they would laugh and chide and say we had forgotten the true language of the North. Some old folk say the young people are just brown white men. Like a dog turd that had been out in the weather. Yeah, and young folk get pissed off at that kind of talk, and if they got a few beers or whisky in the gut, they might fancy to punch someone in the mouth or yell or bust things up, just for the hell of it. The trouble is, of course, me and many like me have not forgotten the so-called true language. You can't forget something you never knew.

"You know, most of us went away south to school. You don't learn the old language down there. But shit, we know more words than anyone else! I do. Lots of words. Democracy. Land rights. Pipeline. Drilling rig. Roughneck. Torque wrench. Hydrogen bomb. Revolutionary struggle. Johnnie Walker. Cunnilingus. Lots and lots. So who gives a damn how many words you got for snow or seals or what the hell? Who cares about what is the right name to give a dog when anybody can go buy a Ski-doo? Who gives a shit? Well, I'll tell you. Me. That's who. That's why I always listen to the old people and try to get the inside, heart meaning of the words. Because there is real meaning, and we'd better get hold of it, quick. When old people think you want to listen, and not just make fun, some of them can surely explain things the way they need to be explained. It's a pity they didn't get it all written down in books.

"I had an uncle, you know, a real old timer. He only moved into the town twelve years ago. His father, my great-uncle, died out in the camps, and they buried him on a hill, under rocks, just like they always did. They say the old man was an *angakok,* a shaman, a magic man. I never met the old fellow, but my mother says he had real power. He could do this telepathy stuff you see on the TV, and he could speak to animals. That's a fact.

"Anyway, my uncle Ooniak was the one who taught me how to make snowshoes, use a dog whip, fix up a .22 so you could hit seal with it. He even taught me how to make snow houses. When them CBC [Canadian Broadcasting Company] guys came up to the Eastern Arctic last year, it was me and one other older guy who built one for them. We were the only guys who could build an igloo real fast, and strong enough so you could stand on the roof afterwards. They showed it on the television down in the States.

"Uncle Ooniak learned most of the real old ways from his father Ipeelee. He knew more than any of these university professors. He never got to speak good English, so the only job he could get around town was emptying the honey bags out of the crappers in the government houses. He didn't mind, though.

"He was a fine carver, and could have made lots of bucks, but he didn't bother. I really respected that man. Out in the bush (that's dumb you know, calling it the 'bush'), Ooniak could really get around. When he went out, he used to come alive. I often wondered what he was thinking, in the last years before he died, coughing up spit and blood because he wouldn't go south to the hospital. He used to stand outside the house, watching the cars and the Ski-doos and the young people coming home drunk, talking English all the while, fighting, not knowing the difference between a male seal in rut and a yearling. Uncle Ooniak would just stand and watch, his face quite bland, as if he didn't give a shit, while all the time, in his mind, he was going over and over the changes to our people.

"But that guy, he never hated anybody, not even the snotty-nosed *Kabluna* with their expensive dog teams they had to feed on imported dog chow 'cos they ain't never going to get any seal. No, he never hated. He would always smile and take time to show them how to space their dogs, use a whip, fix harnesses. If they asked him, he would even go out with those white jerks once in a while. The whiteys used to say he was a 'good Eskimo.' Shit.

"He was, though. Uncle Ooniak was one of the best. Once I told him how we young Inuit loathed the *Kabluna* and would one day throw them out of the North, them and their fancy Mickey Mouse welfare dog crap. Condescending bastards. Boy, old Ooniak got so mad at me and started pointing at my clothes and shoes and cigarettes and everything in the house, saying that I took all these things from the *Kabluna* because I had no soul, like an old whore fucking for a couple of beers. Yes, he said it, and that was the day I really began to try to listen and learn, because I realized that once he and the like of him were gone, we would lose so much of the knowledge that allowed our people to belong to the land. Those were his words too, that we Inuit belonged to the land, not that we owned it. I got interested in everything he said, all the old legends, everything.

"There was one story he told me about his father, Ipeelee, and this white kid. The story didn't make sense to me at the time, and it still makes me think. Then I heard the same story, in different places, told in different ways, changed in the way that old folk change things just by the way they say them. The story is a kind of legend now.

"A bearded fellow came up from Ottawa. He could speak our language, you know, and he wanted to tape all the old stories he could and get them into a book. Well, he made the book, with the stories written in English and syllabics, with pictures made from soapstone prints. I really like books. I don't care if people laugh. Well, I got this book here and I'm going to read a bit out of it."

Before the day the *Kabluna* came and lanced all the great whales and killed them, and then speared the body of the earth so deep that its blood ran thick and black, there was peace on the earth. Luma, the sea goddess, and Raven, the *sila* of the earth, looked into the future and saw what would happen. They knew they must do something and talked about getting ready to save the earth before its blood ran out. For a

long time, Luma had been angry because of the whales, and
rarely talked with Raven. However, they knew they must
find a man who would be strong and wise enough to stop
this bleeding. Luma said the man must be Inuk, for the Inuit
are of the sea and understand its wisdom. Raven said no, it
had better be *Kabluna*, for they knew the magic of iron and
air and machines. They quarreled and quarreled until the
Old Man in the Moon came down and said the man they
must find should be both Inuk and *Kabluna*, for he would
need magic from both sides, and enough cunning and deceit
to be able to disguise his powers.

Luma and Raven agreed and sent for Toodlik, the loon, for
she could fly over the land and dive deep into the sea. They
asked Toodlik to search for a man, half Inuk, half *Kabluna*.
Once he was found, this man would plug the wounds in the
earth and clean it of scars, and he would stop the fighting that
must surely arise between Inuit and *Kabluna* as it did in the
days of the dog-men. Toodlik set off to search, and is still
searching, crying out to find this magician, wherever he
may be.

"The book was written five years ago, and got a lot of press,
and lots of people said he was making it up, because nobody
would see any fighting between Inuit and whites, and nobody
had heard the story before. Well, that was bullshit, because
all the Inuit in the East knew that story, in one form or
another.

"Uncle Ooniak told me that his father's father had dreamed
that story, long before they even heard of oil wells and pipe-
lines. He also told me that he had known a white man, a real
white man from England, who became a shaman and then
got shot by his own people for it. Uncle Ooniak said that they
never found the white guy's body because Luma took him
down into the sea with her and kept his soul safe in her

amautik. He reckoned that one day Luma would let the soul out and magic it into the body of a new-born baby, one that was half white, half brown, and that his baby would grow to be a leader for all Northern people.

"They laugh at the old folks and their legends, but I hope there is some truth in that legend about a leader who could stop the fighting and the killing of the land and sea. For sure, we know the fighting started. That's why we had to come here, from our homes all over the North, just to have this meeting about the trouble blowing our way. Yeah, we know.

"Charlie Apeetik and me went to school together. Now he's dead, because the Mounties hunted him down by helicopter and shot him. Maybe they had to, maybe they didn't. They say he was the one who dynamited the pipeline, and I know that for years he said he would do that if they didn't listen to us. I think it's pretty certain that Charlie Apeetik was the guy who went up to that oil rig, kicked the mess hut door open, and shot five men, four of them white and one Inuk. So I reckon it would be good if we started to believe in those old things, and I reckon it would be good if Toodlik the loon got her shit together and found this fellow she's looking for, real quick. And that's all I'm saying for tonight. I got to talk to Charlie's mother."

— Billy Toby, Eastern Arctic representative.
Taken from transcripts of opening remarks
of an emergency meeting of the Inuit Tapirisat,
May 1980, Tuktoyaktuk.

⌐ ONE ⌐

Below, on a hill, a man-shape with tracks in the snow that wind away behind him. He is a mere speck on the vastness of the tundra, and his tracks are a long and squirming tail. He is young, eighteen, broad in the shoulder, blue eyed, dressed in a caribou-skin parka of the Inuit but with trousers, boots and goggles of his own race. Droplets of sweat cling to the soft, brown hairs on the young man's face and turn white in the cold. A frost halo circles the sun, and glittering false suns mark three points of its circumference. Under the spring sun, the snow crust is hard, its crystalline structure altered by daily fluctuations in the temperature. It glitters on rolling tundra hillocks.

With each step of a snowshoe, the crust broke with a crunch. The young man stopped moving. Silence became a ringing in his ears, an awful depth of silence that played tricks with time. He looked around and shifted his mittened grip on the .22 rifle. Distant hills lost their neighbors in a pale blue haze, with the visibility so good he could see the coastline, more than sixty miles away. As he stood still in the silence, he became conscious of the workings of his body, of the singing of blood in arteries and veins, of the rhythmic sigh of breath, the pulse of heart and the ceaseless toil of entrails. Haaaaaaaa! Breath, falling behind in clouds.

Overhead, the sky was a great blue bowl with feathers of cirrus, scratched as if on lamp-smoked glass. His prints behind were monster tracks. Strange invisible *tornait,* Inuit demons of rocky places, trailing him to hunt his soul. Aiyah! He squinted his eyes and flicked his eyes from one sun-warmed, rocky outcrop to the next.

The throaty cackle of a cock ptarmigan echoed in the quiet. The partridgelike bird flew up and alighted on a rock right ahead of the young man, the white of its plumage stark against the darker rock. There were quite a few of these birds around, with the males pompously laying claim to territory, cackling at circling foxes from their rocky vantage points, or strutting over the snow, pecking for berries and willow shoots.

With a small puff of feathers, the lash of the .22 bullet cut through the bird's neck and knocked him out of sight behind the rock. The man trudged over and picked him up, feeling the warmth and plumpness of the breast. The color of the bird's eye wattles was the same as the little speckles of scarlet blood on the snow. The young man pulled out a handful of tail feathers and scattered them in the air, but he had forgotten the special words of old Ipeelee, who was the father of Ooniak. Thus, he had been taught, the soul of the bird would go free. The young man did it a little self-consciously, just stopping himself from glancing around to see if anybody might watch and ridicule him. He took his knife to cut open the crop. He mixed the mess of winter-frozen berries and new willow shoots with a handful of snow. The mixture was a cold, bitter sweetness, and despite what he had thought at first, he had really come to like it.

In the sealskin bag by his side were four more ptarmigan and a white hare. Silence enveloped him. He tried to listen to it, feeling as if he could reach out and pluck it from the air. He had been walking now for five hours, and small rivulets of sweat ran down his chest. Enough.

Like long black cats, the shadows were stretching out from the foot of each outcrop and ridge. Time to go back. He followed the wind-bared ridges wherever possible, feeling the game bag bump heavily against his hip, thinking of modest things he could say if any of the Inuit hunters said anything to him about his small success.

From the top of the last hill, he looked down at the faint smudges of yellow light that came through the heavy canvas of a cluster of tents that huddled some fifty yards inland from the dark blue lines of the tide crack. Just offshore the open water leads wove like veins across the great white plain of Hudson Bay. Dogs howled. As the young white man came into the Inuit camp, somebody called his name, or rather, the name they had given him, and he grinned and waved, but couldn't yet see who it was.

"Tikkisi," called another voice, this time using the Inuit pronunciation of his own, white nickname, and he looked and saw a young girl, Annie, sitting outside a tent and scraping a fresh seal skin.

"Hullo, Annie," he said in English. Somebody else called out to him, and he answered and felt good. The people always seemed happy and interested when a person came back. It was such a welcoming feeling.

Laughter came from one of the tents, and he could hear the muffled crackle of a fire of driftwood, bones, and blubber, blazing away in the steel-drum stove and sending clouds of sparks up the tin chimney. Toward the shore the silhouettes of sleds, harpoons, drying racks and kayak stands stood out gaunt and black against the vivid orange and red of a char-belly sunset. Ooniak's baby son was yelling in the far tent. His yells rose above the murmur of conversation and the faint chords of an accordion. Wind hummed in the taut wires of chimneys. Sea ice grumbled as it shifted with the falling tide.

The young man unstrapped his snowshoes and beat the snow out of his parka and trousers. He slid the unloaded gun into its canvas case, propped it up outside the door of his pyramid tent, and crawled in through the sleeve.

Within minutes the Primus was roaring under a panful of ice, and the lamp was lit. He crawled out through the sleeve again to prepare a couple of the birds for his supper. Being too lazy to pluck them, he skinned them swiftly, gutting them with his fingers and tossing the entrails away for the ravens. Cooking was a chore he always enjoyed. Within forty minutes he would have a passable stew, cooked in a pressure cooker, and he would have enough left after supper for a meal the next day, that is, if he didn't get greedy and wolf the lot, as he usually did.

Forty minutes. That gave him enough time to sit in the steamy warmth of the tent and go over the three birds to see if there were any lice or external parasites. Somebody in the university in Montreal wanted the damn things. He set out forceps, specimen tubes, labels, a pencil and some alcohol. This was the best part of the day, relaxing, listening to the friendly noise of the stove and the gentle hiss of the cooker, doing the kind of zoology that was really of another era, a far more leisurely era of gentleman naturalists. He wrote as neatly as he could in his field book. "April 29, 1958. Rock ptarmigan

(*Lagopus mutus*), male. Total length 397 mm. Weight . . ."
Whew! The tent was getting too warm, and he had to stop
to tie open the sleeve door and allow the warm air and steam
to rush out. The stew smelled good.

When he had finished his measurements, he went outside
with the carcasses to cut off their heads and to stow them away
where the ravens or a loose dog could not get at them. Philip,
his boss, now absent, was a kind of pack-rat zoologist, with a
large collection of whitened skulls, bugs in tubes, guts and
other things in bottles, dried and spread wings of birds and
bats, shelves full of fossils and seashells, racks of pinned and
desiccated beetles, butterflies, moths. Going into his study in
Montreal was like entering the den of some old wizard. You
expected to see an iron cauldron boiling on the hob or some
damn thing, instead of a big, bearded scientist, working at a
microscope or measuring the fragile bones of a bird skull in his
strong, brown hands.

The young man had an idea about the remaining birds and
the hare. Nobody had asked him if he had got anything, and
he was a little disappointed about that, so he walked over to
Ooniak's tent and hung the presents on a nail above the plywood door.

Ooniak was the nominal leader of the camp, a man somewhat older than thirty and younger than forty, short in the
leg and broad in the shoulders, with a smooth, rounded face
which was slightly squared by his powerful Inuit jaw and
tanned almost to the color of mahogany by the glare of spring
sun off snow and ice. Ooniak heard him, he always did, and
came out sleepy eyed and grinning.

"Would the hunter drink tea?"

"No, this one cooks meat, over there." He pointed back to
his own tent. Ooniak smiled and took down the game, calling
his wife. From within the tent came the loud snores of

Ooniak's father, old Ipeelee. The baby had stopped crying. It was about eleven-thirty at night.

Back in the tent the stew was done. With his boots and duffel socks hanging up in the roof, he sat on his sleeping bag and air mattress and spooned food into his mouth. He enjoyed his own cooking, and it was a hell of a lot better than it had been on his first expedition, which he and Philip had been on together. He emptied his tin plate and poked around in the pot with his spoon, extracting a leg from the stew. He chewed off all the meat and held the bone up to the light of the lamp. There had been bony slivers in the muscle, and they stuck out from the leg bone, frayed ends.

"Ossified tendons," he said, loud and pretentious. It was the first time he had spoken to himself that evening. The sound of the word "ossified" pleased him. It was the kind of word that leant itself to nonsensical associations. He said it again and giggled. He liked fooling around with words.

He put another pan of water onto the stove for the washing up. He even enjoyed that, getting pleasure from all the small, domestic things of his camp life — darning socks, tidying the tent, sharpening knives, writing notes, cleaning guns, filling stoves, waxing skis, tightening snowshoe bindings. It all made him feel rather efficient and assured, and there was so much of it he couldn't have done at all two years before.

Not caring about time, he sang as he washed the few dishes. "Troubled in mind, I'm blue, but I won't be blue always. . . ." He'd been singing that one several times a day for two weeks. It was his habit, to take one song and sing it to death, or just to sing without thinking, over and over, until the words became unwords, nonwords, gibberish, simple sound patterns. He was actually more Welsh than English, having been born there, with Welsh parents. He had a clean, strong tenor voice, and he knew it, and liked people to hear him. He had an extraordinary facility for remembering words even without knowing their meanings. Maybe that was because as a child he had been surrounded by not only the English language, but by the musical, lilting, ancient tongue of Cymry: Wales. In just over a month he had absorbed much of the Inuit language, and exchanged greetings and formalities without knowing or understanding the meanings, but only the times and situations when such words were used.

He wondered how much longer before he would have to give up this fine life in Ooniak's camp? Philip would come north soon, and he would have to leave. Wouldn't it be great if . . .

They were supposed to have come up together, Philip and he, but Philip's baby daughter got sick, and besides, there was a lot of work at the university. Philip had been glad to get the intense and boisterous young man out of the way and to let him come north alone with instructions to ready the equipment, and, if possible, to get it taken by sled across the eighty miles of sea ice to the islands out in the bay. But that had proved impossible, for breakup had started early, and storms had shifted and broken up the floes. This had been a great disappointment to the young man, who strongly felt the need to prove himself to Philip, the man above all others who could, when he wanted, make him feel small and childish and useless.

Philip was inclined to be picky and even ill tempered about small failings. The trouble was that Philip was usually so bloody good at everything he did, and was intolerant of others who couldn't do the same. Physically, Philip was striking. He stood six feet, four inches; he was heavily muscled and a fine all-around athlete. His hair, Saxon blond, hung down to his shoulders in a period when few men wore hair so long. It might have caused him to have been labeled effeminate, had it not been for his huge frame and a thick, blackish brown beard. Philip's facial features were almost delicate, but large, with a straight, fine nose and the palest blue eyes. His voice was odd, strangely high and almost feminine at times, but with a peculiarly penetrating quality. It was a strong voice, capable of filling a lecture hall with ease.

The young man — he thought of himself as a young man, although the Inuit name for him was "Boy-who-smiles" — was a fairly impressive physical specimen himself. He was just short of six feet tall, with a wrestler's chest and arms. In England, he had spent much of his free time over the past five years at wrestling, judo, and fast-water kayaking. He always kept his hair short, thinking he looked tougher that way. The sparse fuzz that the weeks up north had produced on his chin was a disappointment, but he kept it anyway. He was tough though, and Philip was the only man, except for his wrestling coach and the stocky Japanese judo teacher, who had ever managed to hold him down, or defeat him in feats of strength.

The young man's "real" name was Richard Tavett. His family called him Richard, or Rikki, and a long time ago in school, when the class had been reading Kipling, somebody had called him Rikki-tikki Tavett. After that they called him Tikki, which became shortened to Tik. Many people down south thought Tik was his real name. He liked it. It was different.

Tik was emotional, made and lost friends easily, and had respected few people deeply until he met Philip, and then, of course, the Inuit.

Tik had met Philip when he was fourteen, and from that day on, the man had loomed very large in Tik's life, so much so that even his speech habits, mannerisms and philosophies had became molded to the older man's example.

It was very much against the wishes of his parents that

Tik had quit school, worked at odd jobs, and saved up enough money to come to Canada on their first expedition into the Canadian Arctic the previous year, 1957. It had been hard on the lad, but he had grown fast and become a fairly good field biologist. This was the second expedition, and Tik had been very keen to prove to Philip his reliability and resourcefulness. Therefore, when it had proved impossible to make the over-ice journey to the islands, Tik had felt that he had failed. The sense of failure was magnified by the fact that just two weeks ahead of him, another scientist from McGill University had made the journey with two sleds and dog teams, just before the shifting, breaking ice had made it impossible. Like Philip, the other scientist, a Canadian named Clyde Walker, would spend the summer doing research out on the remote group of islands that had not been discovered by white men until the 1930s.

Tik had cursed and raged, not looking forward to a long wait at the settlement, and knowing that nobody would get over to the islands until the ice had cleared off the lakes enough to allow a floatplane to land. That might take as long as two months. He wrote back to Philip and told him not to come. He didn't want Philip to come, not yet. Although Tik still made a hero out of Philip, Philip was impossible to live with if circumstances frustrated him.

So for a few days Tik had stored their equipment and made it ready for a plane flight, then wandered disconsolately around the untidy bleakness of the settlement, with its government buildings, school, clinic, radar site, airfield and the ramshackle huts of the settlement Inuit. However, his bad luck was to change for something that was to make life more exciting than it had ever been before.

Tik had made friends with the Anglican missionary, whose small wooden church served both Inuit and white in the settlement. It was through this man, who had been impressed with the young explorer's interest and enthusiasm, that a band of Inuit hunters from an outlying camp agreed that Tik could join them. The hunters had come in to sell their winter haul of white fox pelts at the Hudson Bay store, and to buy supplies and ammunition for the spring seal hunt. Tik traveled back with them, taking with him a tent, camping gear, a folding kayak, stores of food for himself, and a large amount of flour, sugar and tea to give the hunters who had accepted him.

Once he had set up his tent at the campsite, some thirty miles down the coast, he had been overwhelmed by the unabashed curiosity of both children and adults, who took turns to crawl into his tent and examine his gear with loud comments and exclamations, and not a little laughter. For a while he had been irritated by that, wanting privacy, but he soon realized that this was the way of the people. Then one day, he had taken a walk up the hill to escape the ring of grinning people who would surround and watch him at whatever task he was trying to perform. From the top of the hill, he looked down on the campsite, at the five big tents of the Inuit, each with its smoking chimney and plywood door — big tents, half in the design of a ridge tent, yet rounded. They were double walled and large enough for a family. These were the spring and summer dwellings of the hunting people, sewn by Inuit women themselves from canvas bought at the settlement store. Tik looked from those tents to the green, pyramidal shape of his own tent, so different. Then he understood that he himself was different, a curiosity, and it was no small wonder that the people crowded around to poke through his things and watch his every move. He laughed out loud to himself, and walked down the hill feeling a lot better about the whole thing. With his acceptance of their open curiosity, the people soon accepted him.

It got busy around the camp. The hunters were out after seals that swam in leads that were opening in the sea ice to the east and north. The women were kept busy flensing and stretching the skins, and Tik loved to watch them. One day he got young Annie to show him how to take the fat and scraps of flesh off the stretched skins with the *ulu* or half-moon-shaped woman's knife.

On his fifth day out at the camp, Tik got a seal. It was luck. He had been able to creep up on a seal that was basking by a crack in the ice close to a high ridge of pressured ice that gave Tik cover. The seal was a yearling, inexperienced, and it paid for its lack of caution in choosing a basking spot, with a bullet through its head. Tik came proudly into the camp, trying to be nonchalant, carrying the seal over one shoulder. Ooniak, the camp leader, had been loud in his compliments, for he saw that the young man carried only a .22 rifle, and when told that the seal had been shot on the ice, and not in a lead, he had been much impressed, for seals were generally very difficult to stalk over the ice. Tik was a little deceptive over the circumstances of the kill, not mentioning or describing the pressure ridge which had given him cover. Ah well.

On other days he would shoot other seals, but he would do so in the water of a lead, where the hunter could wait for the animal to surface, and then after killing it let wind bring the floating body to the edge of the ice where it could be hauled out. That was much easier hunting, and even ten-year-old boys did that.

Tik thought that with the kill of the first seal he had won the respect of the Inuit, impressing them with his skill. In truth, however, the hunters and their wives had seen how filled with pleasure he had been when he came back to camp, and had been happy with him, but they had also laughed at him, for in carrying the seal the way he had, like a sack of flour on his shoulder, he had dirtied his anorak with blood, like a child. A hunter would have passed a thong through the seal's jaw and dragged it home over the snow, letting the ice crystals clean the pelt, and keeping himself clean too. But the young white man was such a happy, grinning child that they shared his happiness, for they always like to share happiness.

Ipeelee, Ooniak's father, saw all this and saw too that the boy had an affinity for the land and the sea, an affinity that had been cramped, not allowed to develop. The boy knew little, and was clumsy, yet was forever eager, interested, and not given to the continual garbled noise and crude joking that white men seemed to think was talk.

Old Ipeelee had much he wanted to say to the boy, but he had no English, and Tik's command of the Inuit language was very rudimentary. How then could a man of power speak of things so subtle and difficult as the stopping of time, as how to reach out to touch the dreams of a basking seal, a caribou, or a bird, or as how a hunted animal could sense immediately the pushing, greedy, impatient and irreverent thoughts of a hunter who had not been taught these things? But Ipeelee knew that even though he might not be able to reach the boy, he would eventually find a way. Yes, he thought, there was promise in the eyes of the boy, for they caught the light of sky or ground or ice or sea, changing color in a manner that no Inuit eyes did, yet they were open and honest and malleable, giving Ipeelee confidence in his eventual influence over him.

One clear morning, very early, Tik was called from his tent by young Annie. She told him that her grandfather waited for him, and gave him a canvas bag of warm bannock.

Tik hurried to the jumbled ice at the tide crack and picked his way over it to the smoother ice beyond, where Ipeelee waited with a lightly laden *komatik* and seven dogs.

"This one sees Tikkisi," he said, then walked around the boy, scrutinizing his anorak, duffel socks, high boots and mittens. It was good that the boy did not wear noisy, rustling nylon.

"Eyes?" he asked, so Tik took a pair of sunglasses from his pocket, and the old man nodded. "It is good. Today we go hunting."

"At the leads?" asked Tik, glancing into the distance where the gray of water sky banded the horizon.

"No," came the answer.

The dogs, impatient to go, were making that strange strangled noise that a husky uses for a bark. They looked back at Ipeelee as he checked the lashing on the *komatik*, tugging and puffing and muttering to himself in the warmth of his caribou-skin parka. Satisfied, Ipeelee cracked a long, walrus-hide whip over the heads of the dogs, and they jumped up and threw their weight against the fanned traces, jerking the sled forward with ease, and setting off at such a pace that Tik was left behind. He sprinted hard to catch up, and Ipeelee yipped a command for the dogs to veer west, emphasizing it by laying down the whip on the opposite side. Panting with the sudden exertion, Tik came alongside.

"An old man must ride," shouted Ipeelee against the wind, "but a young hunter should run." So Tik ran, his legs pounding, and his heart leaping at the excitement of it, at the swift skimming of the long wooden runners over the ice and snow, and at the rhythmic panting of the dogs, who seemed to run with as much joy as he did. Far out they headed, westward, where the ice was still firm. The land receded from them.

Ipeelee let Tik run for an hour before indicating to him that he too could jump onto the *komatik*, which Tik did, gratefully, his chest, belly and back slick with sweat under his parka. The dogs slowed to a steady, leisurely pace.

Three hours out from camp Ipeelee called softly to the dogs and they slowed down to a walk. Tik jumped off and pointed excitedly to several dots way out ahead of them: seals. Ipeelee nodded and smiled. Yes, yes, he had seen them, twenty minutes earlier. The dogs came to a halt, and with pink tongues lolling, flopped onto the snow, one of them nipping at a flea by the base of its tail, and another one trying to start a half-hearted quarrel with an older dog, which ignored it.

Unhurriedly, Ipeelee slid his .303 Lee Enfield rifle from out of the sealskin sheath, jacked a shell into the breech, and slipped the safety catch on. He took his rolled-up hunting screen, a square of white canvas stitched to wooden slats, and made it taut by sliding the notched center slat into place. He held the screen up and said its Inuit name, *tadloak*, twice, until Tik repeated it, then gave a glance at the dogs and at the nearest dots, more than half a mile distant. He spoke one more word to Tik.

"Wait." Tik sat down on the *komatik* and chewed on a piece of bannock, watching as the old man stalked toward a seal, moving a few yards at a time each time the seal's head went down in a doze. The stalking seemed to take ages, and to Tik it appeared that old Ipeelee was close enough to the seal to reach out and grab it by the tail. Eventually a shot echoed across the glaring white plain, and Ipeelee stood up. At the sound of the shot, the dogs jumped up and began to pull the sled in the direction of the old man, who was now walking over to the dead seal, which lay with its bloody muzzle over the lip of a round hole in the ice, the back of its head shattered.

When Tik and the meat-eager dogs reached the place where

the dead seal lay, Tik paced out the distance to the place from
which Ipeelee had knelt behind his screen and fired. Two
hundred yards. Ipeelee looked up at the boy, whose excitement was written so clearly all over his face. He grunted, and
laid the seal, a plump yearling, on the komatik. The dogs
would have to wait, and they knew it. He looked at the boy
stomping around and wanted to say, "Look, don't go around
on the roof of the sea as if it were nothing but flat white
ground! Tread softly lest you anger the Sea Mother, and see
how the light in the snow changes here, and over there where
the ice is thinner, and where wide rivers flow beneath your
feet, silent and strong, going and coming from places that no
man — except, so the old ones say, the Old Man in the
Moon, who can see everything from up there — can know,
shaping the underside of the ice. "Listen," he wanted to say,
"listen to the sea under us, listen with your heart, for our
ears are too weak to hear anything but the strains and groans
of shifting ice, too weak to hear the cries of the sea spirits as
they sing their songs and spin their tales." He turned from the
seal on the komatik. "The pelt is good," he said. That was all
he said for the time being. He would have to wait for a
chance to make this white boy feel the greatness of the land
beneath him, a land of great mystery and beauty, from which
only seal and walrus, in times of quiet winds and warm spring
sun, were brave enough to venture. Ipeelee pointed out to
other dots, ranging all over the horizon. More seals, dozing
and watching out on the broad, white roof of their dark, deep
world. Aieee! How brave they were! Would any man be bold
enough to sleep on the bottom of the sea?

"Tikkisi should take that one," said Ipeelee, pointing. "It is
young, and sleeps well, and trusts other seals to watch. Go
from this direction, and other seals will not notice you." He
had to repeat the directions, slowly and carefully, indicating

with his hands that Tik should advance only during the seconds that the seal dropped its head in sleep, then keep perfectly still and hidden behind the white screen when the animal's head raised in vigilance for the approach of its most ancient enemy, the polar bear.

Grasping the .303 and screen, Tik made his crouching approach over the ice. It took so long! His knees began to ache, and his back too, but he grew closer and closer, until he could make out the shape of the seal's flippers, and then the ringed pattern of its silvery blue pelt. How loud was the crunch of his boots in the snow! The seal seemed cautious, alerted, and dropped its head for shorter periods, always seeming to look in the direction of his screen. I can't get any closer, he thought, without scaring the animal, and any time now it will go down the hole. The old army rifle felt heavy, and Tik's sunglasses were misting from the warm, moist air that wafted up through the neck of his anorak. No longer. Heart pounding, Tik slowly raised the rifle over the screen and took the seal in the sights. Its head was coming up! He squeezed off the shot, felt the kick of the rifle, and saw the seal hit, twist violently with the impact of the bullet, twitch, and begin to slide. Dropping gun and screen, he dashed for the hole, but just as he reached it he saw the seal slip slowly downward, trailing blood. He almost wept.

The high yipping of Ipeelee's commands to the dogs brought him back from a deep, black mist of despair. The *komatik* came to a stop, and the old man came and knelt by the hole, inspecting the spots of blood. With his finger he indicated a point on his own neck, shaking his head. He made movements with his hand, and yes, yes, thought Tik, nodding dumbly, it must be a shot that kills instantly, lest the seal twitch and slide down the hole.

Ipeelee smiled and brought out a battered Primus stove, which he pumped up and lit in the shelter of a turned-over sled box. "Tikkisi is too hungry," he said, rubbing his belly, "so now we will have tea and bannock, and wait for a while." He pointed around him. Only very distant dots of seals remained. All the others had dived. The gunshot? The sounds of the wounded, dying animal under water? Some other sense? Tik felt chagrined, and filled a billy with snow.

"Seal come back?" he asked, half hoping they might somehow retrieve his quarry, which, had it been a land animal, would surely have been his. Ipeelee shook his head. He made little round rising circles with his fingers. Bubbles. The seal had been shot through the windpipe; it would die and sink.

So they sat and drank tea and ate bannock, while Ipeelee's eyes ranged always over the ice, to the distant line of coastal hills that were now so clear that it looked as if they had been cut out of paper. In the presence of the old man, Tik felt a great comfort. Finally, Ipeelee ground his cup lip down into the snow to clean it and stood up. He unloaded the .303 and took instead a battered old single-shot "Cooey" .22 rifle. Once again he handed the screen and rifle to Tik, who took them in surprise, looking at the little gun questioningly.

"Closer, closer, closer, slower, slower, slower," said Ipeelee, making slow walking movements with two fingers along the wooden top of the grub box. Tik nodded, and smiled. Yes, with the small bullet of a .22, only a good clean head shot would kill the seal. This time he intended to stalk within fifty yards, or even closer, and he didn't care if it took all day, and all night. He pointed to another dot on the ice.

"That one?"

"Good," said Ipeelee, sitting down and taking a piece of frayed dog trace in his hands, turning it over, thinking partly of how to repair it, but also trying to show by his action that Tik should not think of the seal, only of what he did in the stalk.

So Tik started all over again, and he did indeed confine his immediate thoughts to being completely still behind the screen, and to walking slowly and quietly when the time came. He got so close that he could even see the eye of the seal when he fired. This one did not slip down its hole.

Ipeelee came up with the dogs and the *komatik*. He nudged the dead seal with his boot, noting the small, round wound behind the eye. He nodded and loaded the carcass onto the sled.

"This old man is hungry for meat," he said, turning the dogs back toward camp, with Tik trotting beside the *komatik*, feeling a great joy and wishing he had the words to express it.

Tik's seal was eaten that night, and if there was one thing that impressed the Inuit, it was Tik's enormous appetite. He could eat as much as any other man in the camp, maybe more. He could eat huge amounts of meat, any way it came, boiled, frozen or raw. They hooted with delight and laughter watching him try to eat meat the way they did, cutting small pieces off at the mouth with a sharp knife. Tik was clumsy at it, while even the children could do it with skill. They all were sitting in Ooniak's tent, the seal laid out on a board, delicately butchered by the old man. Suddenly, somebody pointed at Tik, and the others roared and giggled with uncontrollable mirth, the children rolling around on the sleeping platform, kicking their legs and holding their stomachs. With a bloodied hunk of meat in one hand and a belt knife in the other, Tik stared around him, grinning self-consciously, wondering what it was all about. Ipeelee pointed at Tik's nose, wheezing and giggling. Tik put his hand up to find that he had cut the tip of his nose with the cold, sharp knife, and because his face was wind chilled and the cut slight, he had not noticed it. Ooniak jumped up, waving a knife, saying that if he cut the big *Kabluna* nose flat, then Tik would have no more trouble in eating meat the proper way. More laughter. Tik grinned, happy to be the center of merriment. They liked him. He knew that.

In the next three weeks, life for Tik was an exciting dream. He ran by *komatik* over the moonscape of sea ice, the day clear and blue overhead, his body functioning true and strong, his face going browner with reflected light, his breath and the breath of the dogs falling behind in clouds, punctuating the speed and movements of the long Eastern Arctic sleds. Sea shapes, dotting the ice, often distorted by mirage into weird black forms that stretched and wove upward and sideways. Sled runners hissing over the frozen waves of wind-carved sastrugi. Stranded bergs, big and majestic as cathedrals, with sun-twisted ice floes all around like surrealistic sculptures. A man became vividly aware of his body here, of movement, of body sounds and body heat, for his body marked his existence in a clear, strange land of frozen water and wide sky. And then, back at the camp, there was a bustling human friendliness, with endless cups of hot black tea, laughter and stories and children's games.

He watched young Annie telling a story with a cat's cradle, and knew he was becoming infatuated with her. She was fifteen, eldest daughter of Tommy, Ooniak's younger brother. The moon-faced and clear-eyed girl invaded Tik's private fantasies when he lay in his tent, dreaming that he could live this way, with the Inuit, forever and ever, especially if he had somebody like Annie, somebody with skin so clear, eyes so alive and brown, hair so black and shining like a raven's wings, and when she smiled at him, which she did more and more frequently now, he felt a longing that was surely more than physical, more than just the allure of her budding breasts and girl-woman hips and thighs.

Ooniak and Tommy invited Tik to go inland with them to hunt caribou. It was a five-day trip, and they got seven caribou. Tik shot two of them with Ipeelee's rifle, which the old man had insisted he borrow. They came back after the hunt with their loaded sled, their dogs straining hard to pull it. Dogs and men were tired after the inland journey, and the men had to heave and strain along with the dogs to help the sled up and down steep ravines, with frequent stops to re-ice the runners. Many times Tik thought that he would surely pass out and lie down on the frozen ground, leaving the seemingly tireless Inuit hunters to go on without him. But he didn't, and he felt so proud at reaching the camp — when children ran out whooping with delight, trying to jump a ride on the sled, and Ooniak laughed and pointed at him, telling the camp that two of the caribou were Tik's, that his eye was good — that he ran with the *komatik* like a man. Aiyah!

At the feast that followed, Tik ate so much, and so soon after the hard and grueling exercise, that he went outside and got sick, his head reeling, the ground rocking under him, while two dogs squabbled to wolf up the vomited meat. Ooniak came out to him and gave him cold water. He said that a man needed much water, that it was better than tea, and that Tik should come back into the tent and try to eat a little more, some boiled caribou tongue maybe? Tik went back in, and Ooniak's wife fussed over him like a mother, and he felt as if he were at home.

Old Annie, Ipeelee's older sister and grandaunt to young Annie, brought out her accordion and played a Scottish dance tune brought to these shores long ago by whalers. Tik ran to his tent and fetched his mouth organ and played along with her, stamping the floor with his booted feet. Old Ipeelee sat by him and slapped his shoulder, saying he should not go back south, but live with the people.

"All winter?"

Ooniak exchanged glances with his father, which showed nothing of what they thought.

"Forever," said Ooniak, "if it is good with you." Pleasure and pride brought sudden tears to the young man's eyes, but Ipeelee saw the flash of a dream that had troubled him, seeing power in the words so quickly spoken.

At that moment Tik thought of Philip. He wished Philip could see him now, see how well he got along with the people. He remembered the time last year when Philip had scornfully said that Tik was too childish and clumsy ever to gain respect from the Eskimos. He'd have to take that back now. . . .

The weeks rushed by. Evenings, so many evenings alone to think, and dream.

Tik finished the dishes and stowed them way in the red-painted grub box. He made cocoa and got into the sleeping bag, leaving the stove on for a few minutes while he sipped the cocoa and wrote in his diary. The smell and feel and sound of all things around him made his skull tighten in an ecstasy of happiness. The clear bark of a fox on the hill cut into the stillness. He turned off the Primus and lamp and felt silence and darkness close in around like a blanket. He zipped the bag up to his nose and squirmed down into it to get into a comfortable position. Tomorrow? What tomorrow? How about fishing for char through the ice on the lake. Sleep would come easily, but it was not long before he muttered and cursed and wriggled out of the bag to go outside and pee again. He always had to do that.

✒ TWO ✒

O n this day, the sun was stronger and the land beneath patched like a quilt where the snows had begun to go. By the shore, Inuit children threw stones and small harpoons at a bladder which was being towed by a boy in a leaky old skin kayak. The little boys held their mouths tight with concentration as they threw, and then, with each hit, their faces broke into smiles and they babbled excitedly. Out on the sea, where the pack ice had been blown away from the land by recent winds, two men skirted the pack edge in their kayaks, hunting seal. With the shifting of the dark ceiling of ice that had allowed light to filter weakly to the waters — weak light that had grown skins of green diatoms on the bottoms of floes yet had not penetrated far into the sea — there came now a brilliance of rays, reaching deep, stimulating phytoplankton and all the myriads that fed on them to explode into life. The sun was back, sure enough.

Hah! Wide-eyed, a seal surfaced, and even as it snorted air, one of the hunters grunted from deep in the belly and hurled a harpoon, letting the line snake out of his left hand. The wounded seal dove in a great flurry of water as the barbed head bit deep into its neck. The line curved down, down, down into the green depths.

"Aiyah!"

As he followed the float bladder moving on the surface, the hunter loosened the killing lance from its thongs by his cockpit. This one preferred lance to rifle. . . .

Inland, by the shore of a lake, Tik prepared his kayak. A single glaucous gull watched from a rock. Bird sounds, water talk and ice whispering everywhere.

From hills and slopes, a hundred small streams trickled and gurgled over rocks, tumbling downward to join larger streams that rushed in their pebbled beds and carved ditches through the shore ice. The combined sound of so many rushing streams and rivers was like the sound of a gale in autumn trees. Funny, thought Tik, no trees. . . . His mind wandered to home, but he pulled it back, pushed aside the memories of sitting by a fire in his living room, going through catalogs, ordering this kayak, taking it down to the Avon, and paddling beside green meadows with their solemnly inquisitive cows. No, it was here, a suddenly present springtime, with old-squaw drakes yodeling for mates. Ah . . . ah . . . ah . . . ah-how-lik . . . and eiders bowing and cooing, and buntings and long-spurs trilling among the rocks. Yes indeed it was spring, not the gentle green spring of Britain, but a dynamic and urgent spring, with wildfowl streaking in like javelins to the widening waters.

By the camp, on a patch of bare ground, two ravens pecked at the sad white shape of a puppy's skull, a puppy that had been strangled last winter to provide trim for a child's parka.

Tik finished tightening the last of the wing nuts in the brass plates that held his collapsible German kayak together.

39

They still shone with the polishing he had given them in Montreal. Part of Tik's immense pride in his kayak was perhaps due to the fact that he was skilled in a kayak, even more skilled than Philip. No, not "even" more — a damn sight more. Using a big flat boulder as a launching dock, Tik eased himself into the cockpit and pushed off.

Like a big pancake, the lake ice was floating in the middle of the lake with a ribbon of water all around it, ten yards or so wide. As Tik paddled around this moat, the bow wave of the kayak caused candle ice to tinkle and rustle. He stopped paddling when he reached his net float and drifted over the silver and green shapes that struggled beneath him. Six, ten, a dozen, fifteen, even more. With a couple of back strokes he slued the kayak around and grabbed the float line so that he could pull it over the splash cover of the cockpit and untangle the fish one by one, quieting the violently struggling ones with a bite in the back of the head, the way he had seen old Ipeelee do it. He wound the dripping coils of nylon onto the canvas of the kayak and hauled up the rock anchor in a cloud of silt. In less than a week, two of these little survival nets had taken over two hundred char as they dodged out from under the ice cover and hit the nets, which Tik had set along the ice edge.

Tik had hauled out his kayak and was swabbing the slime and blood off it when Ooniak sauntered over. He squatted down and picked up one of the fish from the pile.

"Many fish," he said.

"The net is good," answered Tik.

Dropping the fish, Ooniak took one of the nylon filaments between finger and thumb, testing it, feeling the braided lead line and the durable plastic float line. He grunted.

"Too thin."

Tik protested. No, the net was strong. It had caught many

fish. He could carry it in his anorak pocket when hunting, it was so small, and if a poor hunter such as he could not kill meat, then he could just set the net, even by tossing it from a shore with a rock and line, no boat needed.

Tik was sometimes exasperated by the Inuit, even by Ooniak. They seemed so stubbornly conservative at times, and once they believed something was or was not, then arguing with them was quite futile. It was futile for Tik to try arguing anyway, with his slim and fuddled command of the language. And it was the language, he knew, that was the key. It was such a wondrous and complex thing, folding over time and circumstance, weaving intricate lines of grammar and mean-ing, with multilayered realities. To Tik it was a magical lan-guage, seeming now so far out of reach. He felt sad that all he could do was to lay out chopped-up pieces of the language, verbs and nouns and names and things cut and arranged like pieces of meat on a rock.

"Too thin," said Ooniak, enunciating his words clearly for the young white man. "This net will just catch little fish."

Tik shrugged. Ooniak pointed to the fish lying on a patch of snow. "These little ones," he explained slowly and clearly, "they stay in this lake all the time. They do not return to the sea. Never. They live always in this lake. They cannot grow fat. The fish, the ducks, little birds along the shore (and here he made imitations of busily pecking sandpipers and plovers, which made Tik laugh), and men too, us, Inuit, we all grow fat from the sea." He pointed to a jumble of lichen-covered rocks and boulders and said that the river had died there and that the pathway to the sea had closed when one day the sleep-ing giant of the earth had rolled over and raised up part of himself. He was right, of course. The land had indeed risen at some time, causing shifts which had blocked the river, locking in the char. The biggest fish taken from this lake had been a six-pounder, an ugly old cannibal with a huge head and a thin body and a gut squirming with parasites. Ooniak finished his story and sat and smiled at Tik. Tik picked up one of the two-pounders he had caught that day.

"See. These fish taste good."

Ooniak smiled. "We will eat them with a little rib fat from a young seal. Then they taste good. The big fish coming in from the sea are fatter, bigger, better taste."

"A bird in the hand," said Tik, in English.

"Uh?"

Tik then laughed and asked Ooniak if he thought Tik was like a woman, catching little fish while real men were hunting seals. Ooniak laughed too, in the high, giggling way of the Inuit, and said no, Tik was a man, always stiff like a bull walrus, and that in winter all the girls would run and hide. Tik grinned and blushed and wondered if Ooniak thought he liked Annie. He turned his kayak over and threaded a piece of line through the gills of the fish. As he did so, a loon wailed out on the lake. They both looked up. It was the first loon they had heard this spring.

"What is the name?" asked Tik.

"That one is Toodlik," said Ooniak, drawing out the vowel sound to imitate the bird's cry, that sad and piercing sound of evenings, of distant lakes, of camp solitude and old memories, of wood fires and mosquitoes, of many things, of Canada. Tik struggled for words.

"Our language calls that one 'crazy,' like a ghost woman, crazy and screaming, like a wind ghost." Tik imitated the sound and Ooniak did not laugh, but shook his head.

"Toodlik is not crazy. Toodlik is wiser than other birds, wiser and older even than Inuit. Wiser than *Kabluna*, who

have no ears." Tik shrugged. It was only a name. He continued to thread the fish onto his cord.

The ground was now slushy in places, and as they walked
back to the camp, some wetness got through the seams of
Tik's new sealskin boots. Women and children were gathered
around on the beach where old Ipeelee was cutting up a seal.
Tommy and Jobi, his sons, were coming back in the big
freighter canoe, with five more seals in the bottom and their
kayaks laid across the thwarts. The old man looked up and
smiled. Aiee! It was good to have so much meat, and people
to share it with, a new grandchild to sit in the sun. This had
been the first day that the men had been able to take the big
canoe out, although still the shifting pack ice would prevent
them from taking it far along the shore. As for himself, the
old man didn't care too much for hunting from the big canoe.
He still preferred the kayak, which was lighter, easily carried,
silent, bringing a man close to the sea so that he might understand what it whispered to him.

Tik had decided that there was now enough open water for
him to return to Whaler's Bay. He had been in Ooniak's
camp for a month, and it was time he headed back and got
things ready for Philip. Weather was good, despite a bank of
altocumulus to the west. Yes, he would go the next day.

Tik's decision did not please Ooniak. He said that there was
a lot of ice moving around, and that the wind could easily
bring the pack close into shore and jam it there, preventing
travel. But Tik was adamant. He had decided to go, and once
he had made a decision to do something, he was always impatient to do it. Ooniak wanted Tik to wait for a couple of
weeks and travel with him and Tommy, but Tik laughed and
said he would be fine, and Ooniak said nothing more but just

kicked at the wet crystalline snow, puzzling at this young man's constant need to show that he could be like the Inuit, in ways that only a *Kabluna* trying to be Inuit would follow.

"You will take meat with you, and bannock," he said, and walked back to his tent. He came back soon with a lobe of seal liver, Tik's favorite.

"Why do you want to leave this camp?"

Tik stared at him. "No, no, I never want to leave! My friend comes and I must go to see him. He comes from Montreal."

Ooniak knew Montreal. Once, he had been in a hospital there. He hadn't liked it. Tik looked into the deep brown eyes, wrinkled all around with crow's-feet from squinting into the glare off ice, snow, and water.

Tik pointed to himself. "This one wishes to return to Ooniak's camp." He tried to find the words but couldn't. "Ooniak is my father."

The Inuit's eyes widened slightly; then he smiled and shook the young white man's hand. "Good. Then it is true indeed that this one, this Ooniak is your father, and you will return to our camp."

Tik left early the next day, before any of the people had risen from their sleeping platforms. His tent and some gear were packed and would stay until Ooniak could bring them into the settlement at Whaler's Bay. He walked over to the lake and carried back the kayak. His pack and sleeping bag he stowed inside the little craft, and his rifle in its case went up front. Before leaving, he made a mental check — some dried food, a little meat in a billy, three fat, round bannocks made for him by Ooniak's wife, a little tea and sugar, a small stove and fuel, matches packed in wax, spare clothes, a survival net, ammunition. And as he finished his mental checklist, he thought, "why do we *Kabluna* always carry so much stuff, even when we travel light?"

Waves lapped against the smooth rocks of the beach. Marching before each swirl of a paddle blade came the drip circles of water drops as they fell from the plastic drip guards. Left arm, right arm, left, right, left, feeling strength in his belly the way old Ipeelee had said, banishing fatigue with a mind-poem or a song, a song not sung out loud but whispered inside, and the kayak gliding forward and forward with gentle, rippling whispers.

Far, far out on the edge of the pack ice were dark dots. Seals? No, too many, they must be birds . . . guillemots?

Sleep was washed from his brain by the cool morning air. He would paddle another couple of hours, then go ashore to brew tea and eat a little bannock and cold boiled meat. He felt happy, and the song that he had been repeating in his mind came out of his belly and chest, loud across the ice-dotted sea, echoing from a line of low, rocky cliffs and startling a flock of courting eiders. He was conscious of the flexing of his forearms, the movement of muscles in his upper arms, shoulders, back, chest and belly, and he sang in time to each dip of the paddle, watching the reflections of chevroned water on the canvas hull of his kayak. Thirty-five miles to the settlement. He hoped — and grinned to himself when he realized it — that people there would see him coming in and would realize that he had traveled by kayak, the way the people used to, and the way a few of the old hunters, men like Ipeelee, still preferred.

By late evening, the buildings and tents of Whaler's Bay came creeping around the bend of the coast. As Ooniak had predicted, Tik had had to contend with several patches of broken pack piled close inshore, but he had been lucky, because in all of these spots there had been a beach upon which portage was easy. Otherwise it would have taken him much longer to get there.

On first sighting Whaler's Bay, Tik felt relief, but then a feeling of loneliness clutched at him, making him hesitate to go in. He didn't care if anybody saw him now, and feeling thus, he chose to pull into shore about a mile away, taking a rest that his body didn't need, to eat a little, listen to the hiss of the little gasoline stove, and watch the movements of birds out by the pack edge.

Six weeks had passed since Tik had left Montreal, and as he thought about it, he began again to feel nervous about the way Philip might react. Would Philip be pleased with the many pages of notes about the arrival of birds, the emergence of plants, the hunters' catch, the weather? As for himself, Tik had enjoyed writing all this stuff down, because the seeming need to do so made him observe with more diligence than usual. But there was a difference between them in that Philip was a collector of data, and he had file cabinets and boxes of accumulated notes, most of which would never be published, or even consulted. Tik felt that this was a way of sweeping the world under a carpet, filing it, boxing it, tidying it up, and for Tik's untidy, bubbling imagination, this was cold, almost alien. He remembered one of Philip's loud complaints on their expedition the previous year, when Philip had yelled at him, "Anyone would think that this was just another bloody adventure, but it isn't. We are here to do some work, to take back something worthwhile, and don't you forget it. And don't bloody well forget who brought you here either!" At the same time, Tik remembered all the preparations for coming north, Philip's obvious excitement, his polishing of guns, sharpening of knives, making of boxes, greasing of boots.

Wasn't Philip even more of an adventurer than he, but trying, perhaps, to pretend otherwise and hide behind all this pack-ratting of numbers and junk? What's the time? asked somebody. Wait a minute, said the other, I have it written here on a piece of paper.

Tik turned off the stove and let it cool. Oh, sure, he would go on taking notes for Philip, and he was glad to do it. Maybe Philip would be able to understand and sympathize with Tik's motives for clearing out of the settlement.

As evening reluctantly pulled in, the lights of the settlement began to compete with the blue wash of sky, and the sound of the diesel generators drifted and faded on the wind. Tik packed his gear and carried it down to the kayak. The machine sounds triggered memories of a film he had seen about British commandos coming by kayak into an enemy port, and he began to elaborate on the theme, making a fantasy in his head. When he reached the settlement landing, he continued to play his game, and was silent about stowing kayak and paddles, glancing around all the time. He had to cross the airstrip, with its searchlight scything shadows from the top of the control tower. The military base, the federal buildings, all those long huts and antennae, fuel tanks, walls, lights on poles — they all seemed hateful and out of place. He pretended he was a guerrilla now, coming down from the hills to attack, and he ran with his .22 rifle across the field, his pack bouncing on his back, until he reached the home of the Northern Service officer. He slept that night in a federal warehouse, feeling, as he listened to the throb of a generator, foreign, divided, out of place.

Morning came, hot and stuffy. Tik was sticky with sweat, and his mouth was parched. He got up and dressed. His shirt smelled of caribou and kerosene, and he needed a shower. He remembered that the NSO had invited him to breakfast, and he began to hurry, wondering if there might be eggs.

At Ooniak's camp, Annie had been embroidering duffel socks, and was sitting on the edge of the sleeping platform in the tent. The wooden door squeaked open and her grandfather ducked in. Annie gave an involuntary little gasp, barely audible, and thought briefly of hiding her work. Ipeelee stared at her and held out his hand. She gave the long socks to him.

"Good, good," said Ipeelee.

"The work is poor," she said, eyes down.

"The work is the best you have ever done, little daughter, though the owner of these feet is large indeed, larger than any Inuit." He gave them back to her.

"This old man has seen. That one, the owner of big feet, is young but comes quickly to manhood. That one too has seen an old man's granddaughter."

She had to ask. "What have you seen?"

Old Ipeelee smiled. "He goes into the houses of the white men with two hearts, one of which he tries to send back here."

"Grandfather, bring him back," said Annie.

Ipeelee gazed at her with generations of past and future sadness hidden behind his smile, and then he left the tent. His knees bothered him sometimes now, and he walked slowly up the hill to the frost-shattered summit. Above, two ravens amused themselves in midair jousts, falling and turning, two black periods on the blue page of the red-edged, night-day sky. Old Ipeelee sat down and took out his pipe.

"Play, little brothers, but when you finish, this old man wishes to speak with you about certain things."

And the short night of late northern spring spread its shawl over the lake-freckled shoulders of the tundra. Ipeelee finished smoking and put the pipe away, now taking out a curiously shaped piece of rock from a birdskin pouch. The rock was flecked with mica. Very softly, he began to chant, staring through and beyond and around the stone until it grew in his hand, vast, and light as a sky, a sky scattered with shards of glittering brightness that shone even stronger than the stars. The raven, for all his blackness, loved nothing as much as things that were light, and bright.

Soon, on a nearby boulder, one raven alighted, soon to be joined by the other one. They cocked their heads, staring at Ipeelee, and he nodded, very slowly.

~ THREE ~

The river moved sluggishly, heavy with silt, spreading a brown fan across the bay where once the tall-masted, reeking whale ships had anchored and sometimes wintered. Close by the banks, out in front of the Hudson Bay Company buildings with their white walls and red roofs, a dominion flag fluttered at the newly painted pole. A group of gum-chewing Cree youths lounged outside the store and made dirty jokes about a girl, and inside the store, by the neatly arrayed shelves of coffee cans, traps, boxes of oatmeal and ammunition, canned pork, and the racks of heavy shirts and parkas, a girl, maybe the same girl that the young men joked about, was wandering aimlessly, picking things up and putting them down again. She had no money. She didn't want anything anyway.

In the back room, where skins were hung or baled in luxurious mounds and cascades of browns, reds, whites, grays, and silvers, a young Scottish clerk graded and sorted the catch of a tall, gray-haired and solemn Cree hunter who stood and waited with silent dignity until it was all finished.

By the river, a boy was plinking at cans with a .22, and

along the road from the airstrip a battered blue pickup truck bumped along trailing dust, with three small boys balancing precariously by the tailboard, shouting and waving, parka hoods down over their brown faces.

Tik stood, his ears catching the drone of a DC3 up above the opaque gray of stratus. To ravens, coming and going, calling and calling in the timeless sky, the airstrip appeared oddly symmetrical in the scrubby, darkish green of the taiga.

Nobody could have been more excited about the arrival of the scheduled flight than Tik — not the pilot waiting for his wife to come up and join him, nor the guys from the base waiting for fresh food and mail, nor the handful of people who were returning south. The two men from the base were fooling around, shadowboxing with each other and whistling at a couple of Inuit girls who waited by the freight office, and who in turn glanced frequently sideways at the tall, brown-faced white man who stood so quietly and who smiled at them with such open kindness.

The DC3 came roaring in, blowing dust off the runway and making the eyes of the men who wheeled out the passengers' gangway blink. Philip was the last one off the plane. He carried a cardboard carton in one hand and a bag in the other, and binoculars and camera cases around his neck. He completely filled the doorway of the plane. Grinning, Tik ran up. They said nothing while Philip took off all the stuff encumbering him and stood waiting for Tik. They both stopped six feet away from each other and then, to the astonishment of other passengers on the runway, both took great sideways leaps, crashing into each other with their shoulders in midair. Philip was heavier than Tik and knocked him over, but Tik rolled quickly in the dust and sprang to his feet, laughing.

"It's getting harder to do that every time, you little shrimp," said Philip, "you've been eating raw seal again."

"Tails, flippers, grunt and all," said Tik, picking up the box on the ground. "How's the family?"

"Fine, fine, they send their regards. Now, can we ask these military men for a lift? Where are we staying?"

"In the transient quarters, federal buildings. Here, here's your pack and kit bag. Just hang on a minute Phil, it's customary to help unload the freight, just to keep on good terms with the locals."

On the way back to the federal buildings, Tik began talking about a dozen things at once, and Philip waited patiently, knowing that in a few hours his boisterous assistant would eventually calm down and begin to make sense. Ah, he thought, it's good to be back in the North again, and gazed past Tik to the white rim of pack ice, half a mile out from shore. He could discern the shape of a freighter canoe, loaded with people and dogs probably, heading in to the settlement.

Philip was pleased with their temporary quarters, which they had to share with two men from the federal government Fisheries Research Board. Like Philip and Tik, they were going to spend the summer on the Beaker Islands, remote, rocky islands about eighty miles offshore.

With a roast of caribou from the NSO's freezer, and vegetables scrounged from a cook at the base, Tik prepared an excellent meal. Back in the department, Philip used to boast of how his assistant was the best scrounger of all, and would laugh about it, telling the other graduate students and professors how Tik would methodically comb through the university garbage, retrieving sample bottles, envelopes, boxes, pencils, and anything that might have any use.

When the meal was over, Paul, the older of the fisheries men, short, bespectacled and Scottish, produced a bottle of overproof rum. Mike, his Canadian assistant, went to fetch a carton of Coca-Cola from the vestibule, and mugs and ice from the freezer. As Paul started to pour slugs of the heavy, dark rum into mugs, Philip covered one mug with his hand.

"Not for Tik, Paul."

"For fucksake," said Mike, who did not really know either of them, "you're not his mother, let him have a drink."

Philip flushed with sudden anger, but said nothing, and the two fisheries men looked at each other. Tik went on washing dishes.

"What about it, Phil?" said Paul quietly, still holding the bottle. "In the British navy, a lad starts getting his tot at eighteen, doesn't he? It sterilizes the system."

"Oh, just one then," said Philip with feigned joviality, "but I don't want my hired hands getting rowdy, you know. Seriously though, Tik is a young athlete, and not used to strong liquor. I wouldn't want him to be sick."

"Yeah, OK, Phil," said Paul, "we'll make it a small one." Paul poured rum into a mug and carried it over to the sink.

"Here you go, Tik. Thanks for the meal, eh, it was great." He winked at Tik and picked up a dishcloth to begin drying dishes, and Tik nodded his thanks for the drink, but in truth he would have preferred to let the whole thing drop. After that, they had coffee and sat around talking, sipping coffee with rum in it.

Tik heard a knock at the door. He would have missed it, it was so gentle, but for the muffled coughing from outside. He opened the door, and there stood Ooniak and Jobi, carrying some of Tik's stuff. Tik greeted them with a barrage of *Inuktitut,* feeling sudden delight again at the way the phrases rolled from his throat and tongue. The two men allowed themselves to be ushered in, self-consciously shuffling their sealskin boots, and looking dwarfish beside Philip who had stood to greet them.

"Are these the people?" asked Philip. Tik said yes. He

shook hands with the two and began talking to them in slow, careful English, thanking them for looking after his assistant. Ooniak and Jobi nodded and smiled and said, "Eeeeee," and took the coffee offered to them, beginning to sweat now in the unaccustomed heat of the room. Paul lifted the rum bottle, now half empty, and looked at Ooniak quizzically.

"No," said Ooniak. "It is not good Eskimo drink."

Tik looked at him. It was the first time he had heard Ooniak speak English, and all at once he felt how difficult it must be for Ooniak, coming into this alien room and seeing Tik changed into an entirely different role. Tik got up and went out of the room, coming back with a piece of antler he had been carving into the semblance of a loon. He handed it to Ooniak who asked for something, a word Tik didn't know.

"He wants a file," said Paul. Tik got one, and watched as Ooniak made a few strokes where the head of the carving joined the neck. The carving took life in the stubby fingers of the hunter.

"That's bloody good," said Philip. "I didn't know you had artistic talent as well as brawn, Tik. But you see, don't you, how he has observed a little better how the loon holds his head."

Ooniak passed the little carving back to Tik. "Good. Now, when you carve, let the bone tell you what is inside it. My father, Ipeelee, always tells us that. It is good, very good." Ooniak stood and smiled at them all again. Both Inuit were sweating profusely now. "Thank you, thank you," he said.

They left and Tik ran out after them, catching up and pressing the little carving into Ooniak's hand.

"Please, give it to Annie," said Tik, and Ooniak looked surprised, and then broke into a tremendous grin, while Jobi giggled.

"Come back to us, Tikkisi, Boy-who-smiles, we will all wait for you," said Ooniak.

Tik watched them go and walked slowly back to the long, wooden hut, thinking about things, and feeling sad and awkward about the hostility that seemed to lie just beneath the surface whenever he and Philip shared the company of other people for any length of time. He went into the room, picked up a mug and the rum bottle, poured himself a stiff drink and knocked it back before Philip could say anything. It was only then that he wondered why it was that the Inuit had come into Whaler's Bay so much earlier, days earlier, than he had expected, and as he wondered about this, the face of the old man, Ipeelee, came clearly into his inner vision. Involuntarily, he shuddered.

As it got late, the others grew red and jolly, but Philip, always a moderate drinker, seemed to become even more aloof and distant. Tik was relating his experiences of the past month, comparing them with those of Paul, who had wintered in Igloolik and traveled with the people there some years before.

"You know," said Tik, "I don't think that the place of a man's birth and culture has all that much bearing on his true nature. For me, I feel so much more at home with the Eskimos than I do back in Britain."

"That's nonsense," said Philip. "You just have a romantic attachment to the idea of being a tough, rugged, polar hero, and if you ask me, you're getting as starry-eyed and wooly-headed as the rest of those fellows at the Arctic Institute, forever talking about the last bear they shot."

"I've never shot a bear," said Tik, and then, realizing that this was a silly retort, he added, "I wouldn't shoot a bear. If I wanted a bear skin, I'd find an old one and follow him around until he died."

"No, no, no," protested Mike, his words slightly slurred now, "what you do is you dig a hole in the ice and scatter some dried peas around, and then, when the bear comes up for a pea you kick him in the icehole." He guffawed at his own joke.

"I don't think I'm a romantic," said Tik, who hadn't been listening to the joke, "not too much anyway, but I believe in what I say even if I can't ever find the right words to express it. I am at ease with the Eskimos; they seem to see what is inside my head, inside my heart, and they don't crowd in on me like people do back in Britain, or down in Montreal. Maybe there is truth in the theories of reincarnation. Maybe I was Eskimo in an earlier life or something."

"Bloody nonsense!" snorted Philip, and they all argued about it, with Tik persisting, and saying that he was thinking of staying on at the end of the expedition, at Ooniak's invitation. Philip shook his big, blond head.

"Tik, that is ridiculous, and you know it. You are going back to college in England. For one thing, you do not have immigrant's status here, but a kind of glorified tourist's visa. For another thing, the Department of Northern Affairs does not let just anybody winter in the north with the Eskimos. They would get the mounted police after you in no time, and you'd get hauled out by the tail like a little puppy dog. Lastly, the Eskimos themselves would not want you around in winter, when they have barely enough to keep themselves alive, let alone a romantic white adolescent with the appetite of an elephant. Quit trying to impress everybody; I know why you're saying all this." Tik colored, and was about to say something angry when Paul slapped him on the shoulder.

"Go back to school, Tik, but keep in touch. Write us next spring and we'll get you north again." He looked sideways at Philip, "That is, if Phil doesn't hire you."

There it was again. Paul didn't stress the word "hire" but Philip caught it and was silent. Of course, he didn't pay Tik. He didn't have to. It was an item of contention between Philip and others in Montreal. The Canadians did not quite go along with his theories that he had every right to make an unpaid assistant do anything, any dirty or difficult job, because a good assistant should be to an expedition leader as a disciple to a guru. Philip had often explained that both he and Tik understood the Oriental philosophies, under which it was common for a young man to choose a teacher, follow him, serve him, and learn by example and discipline in order to be molded by the more powerful personality. Also, maybe the others realized but felt a little exasperated by Tik's seemingly cheerful acceptance of dirty jobs and abuse, for he didn't care what he did or what was said to him as long as he got the chance to go north. Perhaps it was too that in Canadian schools, coeducational as they mostly were, it was rare for that strong bond to develop between a teacher and a student. The conversation lapsed, and Philip excused himself and went to his bunk to read.

A few days later, with an eighteen-foot freighter canoe lashed under one wing of a Canso seaplane, and the aircraft jammed with equipment and supplies, they departed for the Beaker Islands.

With the drone of engines filling his ears, Tik looked out of the tiny porthole in the old aircraft's side, watching the buildings of Whaler's Bay grow smaller. There, stretching to the left and the right, was the dark line of the coast with patches of snow on the north-facing slopes, and in the bay there were white commas of beluga, fifty, sixty, more. He looked away from the window and saw Philip's legs dangling down from the observation bubble under the wing, with his tartan socks tucked into long, well-dubbined boots. With a great yawn, Tik stretched out on a pile of freight and looked down at his own feet, snug in sealskin boots, with the colorfully embroidered tops of duffel socks folded down over the gray and silver top fur. He had found them inside the stuff that Ooniak and Jobi had brought. Must have been a present from Ooniak's wife, he thought. Nice of her. Really nice. He began to doze, knowing that he would not get much sleep for the next few days.

~ FOUR ~

Eider, old-squaw and loon were calling over the wind-tossed lake and laying claim to the small calm ponds. The lakes of the Beaker Islands, like the islands themselves, were longer by several times than they were wide, and in the northern ends of the long lakes, pans of rotten ice jostled each other into oblivion. Over the ridges and beyond, the sea was jammed with floes and small bergs, sometimes piled with pressure ridges. The persistent mechanical hum of the aircraft droned and faded, causing some people from an Inuit camp to come out and gaze upwards, to find the speck against the great expanse of cloud-brushed blue. The aircraft began to circle and descend, passing twice over the lake and miles out of sight of the camp. It roared in over the choppy waves and bounced on its belly like an overfed gull. And then, at the Inuit camp, they could hear no sounds but wind and birds, water and ice.

Tik lurched over his pile of boxes as the plane bounced once, twice, three times. A huge sheet of water crashed over the cockpit, spewing in streams off the windows. Tik steadied himself until the bouncing took on the more gentle dip and bob of wave movement. White-faced, Philip began fussing at Tik to get ready, which was quite unnecessary, for the lad had already begun to unfasten the doors. He scrambled out onto the slippery, wet wing struts and unlashed the freighter canoe. Once in the water, the canoe had to be watched carefully lest it bang against the hull of the plane, and it was Tik who stayed in the canoe while the others handed stuff down to him. He enjoyed it immensely, liked the cold spray in his face and the swinging, bouncing, funfair ride. Philip got angry with him for laughing so much, and nearly slipped and fell into the lake while handing down the awkward bulk of the outboard motor. The pilot too was agitated, wanting to get his plane up and away. It took three trips to transport all their stuff to the shore, and by the time it was done, the plane had drifted so close to the shore that it barely had space to turn and get away from the wave-battered rocks.

It had difficulty, but after a couple of runs, the Canso lumbered into the air and disappeared in the direction of the mainland. Tik and Philip were left alone with the huge piles of wet equipment. The solitude seemed to come abruptly.

"Well, mate," said Philip, suddenly jovial, "I think we deserve a pot of tea before we sort this lot out. You get the stove going and I'll fetch some water."

Sitting on boxes, with their backs to the wind, they drank their tea and enjoyed the treasure of companionship in a wild place, with both of them remembering the many close evenings of the previous summer, and other trips too, in the gentle hills of the Cotswolds and Malverns. Philip picked a sprig of purple saxifrage and stuck it in his woolen cap. He was in a good mood, and didn't feel like hurrying with the chores of setting up a temporary camp. He even talked to Tik about bringing his wife and small daughter out to the islands some time, next year maybe.

They set up their tents for the night, a two-man mountain pup tent for Philip and the larger cook tent for Tik. They never shared the same tent, except to eat in. Tik prepared a meal from cans and set it out in the big tent, while Philip walked down to the lakeshore and stood scanning the little islands and the rafts of waterfowl swimming around them. This was Kasegalik, the lake of freshwater seal, and he was wondering if there would be time in the summer to come back and try to find one. He felt almost affection for his young assistant, remembering Tik's cheerful enthusiasm in the cold and wet, feeling a bit sorry for yelling at him in his own discomfort and worry. What if they had lost some of the equipment, the outboard? What if the sleeping bags had gotten wet? Damn it, the boy never seemed to worry about anything like that. He made a game out of everything that seemed risky or dangerous, and it was infuriating at times. Yet it was good to have the boy around. He hoped, though, that supper would not be served on cold plates in an untidy and unsettling jumble. He could hear Tik whistling. He always whistled off key. In scrubby patches of willow by the lake, black and white snow buntings busied themselves. Supper was almost ready, surely.

Early the next morning they went to explore the far side of the lake and to find the way to begin their journey to Roberts Bay, to the southwest of the archipelago. After a few hours they found an outlet, a narrow channel that fed the swelling lake waters to a swift river. Philip figured that the river would get them to the bay in two or three days of portaging and canoeing. The plane had not been able to land them right in the bay because of ice. Later that day they got into their lakeside camp, and Philip began to divide up canoe loads.

"You'd better test the radio, Tik. Sling the aerial on the tent, it should be good enough for now."

"Sorry, Phil, but it's dead. I checked it last night after you went to bed. Maybe it got damaged in all that bouncing or something."

"What? It was packed in a special box, man. Few bounces wouldn't have hurt it, let me see." Philip looked at the radio box and started cursing. One side had been punched in, and the only thing heavy enough to have done that was the long wooden ridgepole.

"Where did you put this damn radio when you loaded the plane?"

"In the rear."

"I'll bet you bloody well did, and you put the damn bundle of tent poles just in front, didn't you, you stupid oaf. Now we have no communication."

Tik shrugged. "Isolation doesn't bother me. The *Aivit* knows where to pick us up at the end of the summer. Why worry?" He half turned, busying himself with plates and dirty cups. Philip noticed with further irritation that the backs of Tik's wrists were grimy.

"That's just the kind of irresponsible attitude that I hoped you'd learned to better!" said Philip, voice rising. "It bothers me. I have a family, and you don't. Anything could happen. We're separated from people by over a hundred miles of dangerous seas. Damn it, boy, you make me angry sometimes!"

Tik was about to remark that there were Inuit all over the islands, as well as at least two other camps of summer research workers, but Tik hated arguments, especially with Philip.

"I'm sorry. I should have taken more care."

"Damn right you should." Philip got up and walked out of the tent.

Yeah, and stuff your moldy old radio up your bum, thought Tik. He hated the damn thing anyway.

Almost as if in tune with Tik's unspoken thoughts about the lack of isolation, three figures appeared on the ridge behind their camp. They were Inuit, two brothers in their early forties and one cousin who was not yet thirty. Their names were Noah, Danny and Joe, with Joe being the youngest and the self-elected spokesman of the group, because of the three, he had spent one winter in a settlement and had attended the government school there. The brothers, Noah and Danny, had left their native islands only on trading and hunting trips and knew nothing of the language of the white men, nor wished to.

After greetings and handshakes, Joe told Philip of a white man who had come down from the trading post in the north. This white man was now living at their camp, a day's walk distant. The Inuit had difficulty in pronouncing the name, but it was certainly Clyde. Having imparted this information, Joe stared at the ground.

"Teamik?"

"Damn good idea," said Philip, and Tik ran to the tent to boil up a kettle. With a certain amount of ceremony, they all squeezed into the tent for mugs of sweet black tea. A map was produced, and Noah pointed out the position of their camp and the route they had taken. Tik marveled at the seemingly innate ability of the Inuit to read maps without any schooling. As they talked, the map spread over Philip's knees, the tent flap was suddenly pushed aside.

"Well I do declare, everybody is having a tea party. Any room for Alice?"

"Bugger me, it's the Mad Hatter," said Tik, jumping up to shake Clyde's hand. Tanned and healthy, with the crow's-feet on his young-old face accentuated by the deep brown of ice glare and wind, Clyde grinned at their surprise and slapped Tik on the shoulder.

"You're getting pretty hefty for a dormouse," he said, and Tik noticed the good camp smell about him, a smell of caribou hide and seal, of stove smoke and tobacco. Tik handed him a mug, and Clyde hunkered down by the door. He was an anthropologist, Canadian, especially interested in the Beaker Island people. He was doing a thesis on changes he predicted in the life-style of the islanders with the coming into their life of the Hudson Bay Company freighter canoes and outboard engines, which would soon replace the traditional kayaks. The change was sad, but inevitable, and Clyde, whose command of the Inuit language was excellent, wanted to record as much of the old hunting lore as possible before the change. He spoke enthusiastically about the people he lived with, for he had been at their camp for two months now, having crossed the sea ice by dog team before the onset of breakup. He explained that the camp contained thirty or so people, now in summer tents. There were five men in the camp, including himself, Noah, Danny, Joe, and Neviaksi, the camp leader.

"Ah, this one knows of Neviaksi," interjected Tik. "He is the young brother of the hunter Ipeelee."

Clyde and the Inuit looked at him, and the Inuit smiled with sudden pleasure to hear him speak the language of the people.

"That's pretty good, Tik," said Clyde. "You'll be better than any of us soon."

"I was lucky enough to live in Ooniak's camp for a while," said Tik, "and it seemed to bring out all the studying I did with the tapes and notes you lent me over the winter. I've got to thank you, Clyde, really. And I love the language too."

Philip changed the subject. "How's the game situation?" he asked. "Lots of seals?"

"Couldn't be better," answered Clyde, "and I've already spoken to Neviaksi about them keeping seal jaws and ovaries for you, and he's quite happy to do it. I'll need some jars and preservative from you, though.. There's seals, ringed and bearded, beluga, and if you want to head north you'll get walrus. I don't need to tell you about ducks and geese; you can see for yourself. Fish is plentiful too, char by the ton. I tell you, these people are fantastic. True hunters. The best. You know, I even got Neviaksi to build me a perfect scale model of a two-holed kayak! And one old grandma can still make parkas out of the neck feathers and back feathers of eiders. Talk about Joseph's coat of many colors . . . beautiful thing, green and white and black, light and warm, wow, just great, man!"

Clyde, who was several years older than Philip, was one of those lucky people whose limitless capacity for enthusiasm and interest in things around him kept him far younger than his thirty-six years. He had worked for several years in the North for the wildlife service before deciding to go back to McGill and get a doctorate. His thick, curly, black hair was forever disheveled, and although shorter than Tik, he seemed bigger because of his compact, muscular frame. Clyde was the first white Canadian that Tik had met who was truly skilled in a kayak, and for Tik, no attribute, other than perhaps his fluency in the Inuit language, could have been more admirable. Despite their eighteen years' difference in age, they had become pretty good friends during Tik's brief stay in Montreal. Tik tried to persuade the Inuit to stay for a meal, but they stood to go. Joe turned at the doorway of the tent.

"Teamik?" he said.

Clyde looked at Philip, almost apologetically. "They've got no tea, Phil, the last of theirs was finished a month ago." Philip delved into the grub box and handed Joe a fistful of tea bags. Joe paused for a second, put the tea into his pocket, and went out of the tent, with Tik following. The Inuit shouldered their sealskin game bags and took up their guns, old single-shot .22 rifles with the back sights filed down and moved up the barrel and lashed on with wire. Joe stopped again, face serious.

"No bullets," he said.

Tik looked from the rust-pitted gun to the bulging game bags. Joe's bag contained two Canadian geese and three ducks. He pointed at them.

"No bullets, Joe?"

Joe faked an even more serious expression and thrust his hand into his pocket, bringing out a single .22 round.

"One bullet," he said.

Tik looked at them, grinning that wide Inuit grin. He laughed, brought out a box of fifty rounds and gave them to Noah, who said thank you, thank you, many times over.

Clyde volunteered to stay on with Philip and Tik and help them to get their equipment to their planned campsite. Clyde and Philip made the first trip across the lake, leaving Tik in camp to do odd jobs. The air was still, and the whine of their outboard motor could be heard for hours after they set off. Ducks swam on the mirror-smooth water, and small birds chirped in willow bushes all over. The air was fragrant with the scent of saxifrage, and of growing things. Tik hurried through his chores and went exploring, finding a nest of eiders, and capturing and releasing two downy yellow goslings. This was the first time he'd really been alone since his leader arrived, and the discipline and demands of Philip's presence were sometimes hard to take for a lad who wanted often to sit and dream, or to do nothing at all.

That evening during supper, Philip announced that Tik had to come along the next day.

"Oh, we don't need three people," said Clyde. "Why don't you take a day off in camp?"

"We need him," said Philip, and went on eating, his heavy shoulders hunched forward in a pose that was at once protective and tense, as if challenging contradiction. Clyde glanced up with a flash of surprise at Philip's tone of voice, but he said nothing, while Tik made his own irritation obvious by sploshing another ladle of canned stew onto his plate. He didn't like being in a boat with Philip, and he didn't like Philip's protective, almost jealous attitude about his services and presence. And anyway, Clyde was right, they didn't need three men in a boat.

During the night the wind picked up, and by morning the lake had a two-foot chop, making it expedient to lash on the canvas splash cover.

Halfway across the lake, the engine spluttered and died, and Philip, who was at the tiller, squeezed the rubber bulb on the gasoline hose, shook the now-empty tank, and began to curse at Tik. In truth, he wanted to curse himself for a sudden and quite pointless fear, a fear he constantly pushed down, a fear of water. When he had been slightly younger than Tik, Philip had barely escaped drowning. A sailing dinghy had turned over, and he, although a mediocre swimmer, had managed to drag his unconscious companion to the shore, and it was there that the full horror of the situation had struck him. His companion, an older man, was dead of a heart attack, and he had swum for over an hour dragging a corpse. Even now, fourteen years later, whenever he was out on the water, be it sea, lake or river, Philip always felt as if unseen arms were about to drag him under once again, and he remembered the numbing cold of that past experience, the leaden weight of exhausted limbs, the painful retching of a stomach filled with swallowed

THE WHITE SHAMAN

seawater. Philip feared and hated water, and it was curious, if not significant, that Philip had made himself an expert on life in the intertidal zones. Perhaps it was Philip's continuing battle with his own weakness that had made him choose the subject of seals for his postdoctoral work. He considered himself to be a man of ambition, drive, determination and logic, and this, he felt, would at last conquer those old and horrific nightmares.

In contrast, Tik had absolutely no fear of water, and once when they had skimmed the surface of the topic, Tik had said, "No, I'm never nervous of water. How can I be, for most of my body is made of water. Don't you see? Our bodies are full of water that has pretty well the same salt content as seawater, so the sea is our natural element. No, it isn't water that scares me, just cold. Anyway, I float." Back in England, Tik had been a champion white-water kayak man, and a powerful though inelegant swimmer. His father and uncles hailed from a long line of ancestors who had served the British Crown in navy ships since before the time of Nelson. Tik loved the sea and devoured books on the subject, and books about explorers, and about the creatures of the oceans. He saw the sea as the great engine of earthbound life.

The heavily loaded canoe began to swing broadside into the waves, and Clyde grabbed for a paddle. Tik crawled under the canvas splash cover and brought out a ten-gallon drum of fuel, and then went back under for a large funnel and a piece of chamois to filter the gasoline through.

"Sometimes your negligence is just too much," said Philip, going red in the face with the exertion of forcing off a stubborn bung. "You knew we were coming over today, and it didn't even cross your mind to see to it that the gas tank got filled. It makes me angry, really angry. I have to tell you every single

68

damned thing. Why can't you think for yourself?" Clyde had paddled the canoe into the wind again, but it was rough.

"Hell and damnation, man, look at it now!" yelled Philip, as the funnel slipped and gasoline slopped into the bottom of the canoe. Clyde, in the bow, turned and looked at them both.

"Why don't you quit yelling at the guy? And for godsake, you cretin, put that pipe out!"

At this point, Philip was kneeling on a thwart, pouring gasoline into the funnel. His lighted pipe was in his mouth, and his teeth clamped around it in a grimace of anger. He ignored Clyde, who shouted at him again to put the pipe out.

"Phil, for fucksake, don't you know that that's the best way to start a fire in a boat?"

"A fire, in this wind?" retorted Philip scornfully.

"You're damn right! Grab it off him, Tik, before he blows us up. Grab it off him and throw the fucking thing in the lake!"

Tik looked nervously at Philip.

"Just try it," said Philip softly, menacingly, and Tik was shocked, for never before had Philip ever implied a threat to him, and worse at that, a threat based on no reason. Tik looked away.

As soon as Philip was able to shift his grip, he took the pipe out of his mouth and knocked the ashes over the side of the gunwale into the water, muttering under his breath. It took a few minutes to fill the tank through the slowly filtering chamois leather, and things were tense, with all three men angry at each other and impatient to get the motor started again.

Tik took the half-emptied drum and went to put the stopper on the gas tank.

"Get me the blasted oil will you? Don't be so bloody gormless!"

"I mixed oil in that drum yesterday," said Tik, glaring back into Philip's angry, Viking-blue eyes. Clyde shouted again, over his shoulder.

"Phil, will you get off the guy's back and start that fucking thing? It's not his fault we ran out of gas. It was you and I who used the motor yesterday, for fucksake, so we should have checked it. Moreover, you're the Charley running the thing, and you're the one who should have seen that it was full, but more than that I don't give a shit either way if you will stop behaving like a hysterical old woman and leave the kid alone for a change!"

"What do you mean by that?"

Clyde kept his back turned, and continued to paddle with one hand as he raised the other in an obscene gesture. Philip yelled back to him.

"I'll ask you not to interfere with me and my assistant!"

Clyde repeated the gesture and Tik wanted to start laughing. Philip angrily yanked on the starter cord and the engine sputtered into life. Nobody spoke for the rest of the trip across the wind-tossed lake.

For the rest of those few days of travel and portage, Clyde kept his opinions to himself, and Philip did his best to re-establish good terms with him. After all, Clyde was under no obligation to help them, and of course, he was not being paid. To Tik, the tension of that day on the lake seemed to have gone, and they were good days, with happy evenings spent sitting around eating enormous meals, meals made all the more enjoyable by the exertion and expended energies of the hard work. The three men would sit and drink coffee, swapping stories, with the two older men listening half amused by the naiveté of Tik's tales and theories.

On one such evening they camped on a patch of dry ground beside the river, just before a second run of rapids. Clyde had made a quick trip back to the Inuit camp and had returned by kayak with three large char, fresh that morning from the nets. It was the first sea-run char they had eaten that summer, and its delicate pink flesh could not have tasted better. For a long time they sat outside the tents, talking about this and that. Hills and ridges sheltered the campsite on all sides, and the air was warmer and stiller than on the ridges so that vegetation flourished. Willow bushes grew three feet high, and delicate harebells flowered everywhere. As the evening wore on, the two scientists got deeper and deeper into conversation, and Tik found himself daydreaming. The talk was too involved and academic for him. He left them and walked up the side of the ridge, sat down on a rock and began playing his harmonica, enjoying the echoes that made the blues he played sound so much fuller and sadder in the tenuous dusk of the Arctic evening. It was an hour before midnight. Clyde walked up the hill and sat down beside him. Tik stopped playing.

"That's good, man. When we get back to Montreal, you and I should have a session. I'll get out my twelve-string. Hey, I'm going to head back to my camp again, Tik, but I'll be back tomorrow with a few men to help over the big portage. After that one, I reckon you guys can manage. There is just one short portage after that, easy."

"I wish you could stay with us," said Tik. "It's been so much more fun with three."

Clyde stood up. "Yeah, well, work calls, you know. You can manage." They started walking up to the top of a hill, which was in fact the high point of a ridge that caused the river to horseshoe back on itself. Clyde's kayak was beached down on the other side. Tik paused at the top of the hill, awed by a panorama of ribbons and patches of water, glistening orange and silver like necklaces thrown about the land.

"Hang in there, Tik," said Clyde, slapping his shoulder. "Don't let him bully you, you hear? This is Canada, not some snooty private school in jolly old England."

"I'm from a Grammar School," said Tik, not knowing really what to say, wishing not to utter anything disloyal to Philip, yet wanting at the same time to pour out the resentment that had bottled up inside him.

"Yeah, same difference. Don't let him lean on you too much. Tell him to shove it once in a while, and if you want a few days off, come over to our camp, you hear?"

Clyde tousled Tik's hair. Christ, he was a big lad, thought Clyde, but sometimes he seemed as if he were a kid of fourteen or even less.

Tik grinned. "See you."

Tik watched him pick his way down the ridge and then paddle off along a stretch of water that was now blue black, faintly tinged with pink. A solitary loon followed the kayak's course, flying high above, crying with an excited warble, and Tik recalled the sudden fright of his first experience of a loon's cry, last year, in the late evening, when a loon had cried with that lonely eeriness from a lake. Now, a great exhilaration came over him, and all the sounds and colors of this northern land flooded into his being, filled him, raised hairs on the back of his neck. He felt dizzy, wanted to whoop with excitement for all this expanse of freedom shown to him, all these streams and lakes stretched out before him, each with its irregular border of snowbanks, each reflecting the rapidly changing colors of the sky.

Again a loon cried, and Tik believed that he perceived truth in the sound, believed that here was a symbol for him, free and powerful, a sound that echoed all life, filling this great land with power. The loon was Toodlik, and if he had to be named, that was the right name, and Tik felt that within himself were balanced both love and hatred for Toodlik. He felt earthbound, useless, immobile as a stone, and the wild cry seemed to mock his feeble inability to communicate or travel. Would that he could borrow the wings and voice of Toodlik!

"Toodlik," he said out loud, "loon, sky-sword, hit out at the silence, but do not mock me, or I shall have to take you." Then he looked around, shy for having talked to himself again.

He knew that at times, when he felt lonely or sad and feared that he was the last living creature on a dead planet, the cry of a loon would bring great happiness. But now, the loon was a distant black spot, far, far out of reach. Tik would have to hold one in his hands to try to understand.

Clyde returned the next day with the four Inuit men from Neviaksi's camp. They got all but the last load carried past the final stretch of rapids. It was all hard work, but with the Inuit around, good fun. They made laughter so easily, and ran contests with the three white men and with each other to see who could lift and carry the most. Despite their short stature, the Inuit were very strong, with great stamina. They would hoist a ten-gallon drum of fuel, or a hundred-pound sack of flour onto their shoulders with ease, and charge over the rocky ground, puffing and giggling, trying to push each other out of the way. Tik slipped and fell into the river, but managed to keep the bundle he carried above his head dry, and he clowned around in the water, blowing it out of his mouth and whooping with the chill of it. The Inuit laughed so hard they had to sit down. Philip demonstrated his massive strength. He could pick up a hundred pounds in each hand and stride along with a seemingly effortless grace. It was his powerful, relaxed stride that earned him a nickname that day. Noah first gave it to him, pointing at the big man as he carried a box on one shoulder and a ten-gallon drum of kerosene under his left arm.

"The big fair-haired one is indeed strong," said Noah, "strong as Nanook."

So, "Nanook" was the name that stuck, and it was a good one, matching Philip's huge body and his easy, powerful grace, and matching too the shocking blond of his long hair. Nanook — the white bear. Is there truth in the belief that names carry magic? Later, Tik would come to feel that there was, and that when Philip was given the name, "Nanook," his future was altered.

On the last day, the weather turned against them. The bulk of the heavy portaging had been done, though, and Clyde and the Inuit had returned. Just one canoe load had been left up above the final rapids. All the other equipment and supplies were below, piled on the bank and covered with a tarpaulin. From that point, ferrying it by freighter canoe the last few miles to the chosen campsite would be a simple operation.

The cold, gray, rainy gloom of the morning seemed to bring out the fatigue and muscle aches of the preceding days, and neither Tik nor Philip really felt like portaging anymore. Unwisely, they agreed to risk shooting the rapids with a loaded canoe, which might have been fine if either of them had been skilled in handling the freighter canoe, but they were not.

As the canoe began to gather speed, and to swing and cavort with the twistings of the current, Tik, who was in the bow, felt misgivings, but at the same time an excitement, an exhilaration. The canoe gathered speed and they dipped their paddles furiously to try to control it. Halfway down, white water boiled ahead of them, and the canoe started to resound with bumps it was taking on the tops of rounded boulders.

Each time they hit, Tik yelled out, "Ooops!" and although his back was to Philip, the older man again became infuriated. He realized he had made a bad decision, and realized too that although Tik was exerting himself to his utmost, he still did not really care about the situation they were in. Things were getting out of control. The river was playing with them, and Tik, damn him, was enjoying it. Alarmed now, Philip looked ahead to a great wall of boiling water. It hadn't seemed so bad from the bank. The canoe dipped, once, twice, taking water over the bow. A collision seemed unavoidable. The canoe would be smashed!

Tik guessed that they could not paddle clear, and he thrust the long paddle under the bow, thinking to take the shock, or part of it, or maybe to deflect the bow of the canoe from the boulder. But suddenly the canoe swung clear and went helter skelter down into deeper and slower water, with Tik paddling and fending off rocks all the way down. At the bottom of the rapids, in the slower eddies, the canoe began to swing around and around, and Tik shouted back to Philip, demanding that he steer. Receiving no response, Tik looked back to find himself alone in the canoe, with Philip's paddle lying on top of the freight. Frightened now, Tik clambered over the pile, took the paddle and made for the bank. Would he find Philip smashed and drowned in those racing, roaring waters? He tied the canoe to a stout willow bush and walked up the banks, anxiously searching, and it was with relief that he saw the big man climbing out of the water onto the bank, dripping and gray faced.

Philip had seen that they would not avoid the rock, and so, to save the canoe, he had vaulted over the side and used his weight to swing the stern away. It was a foolhardy and unorthodox thing to do, but it had worked. Soaking wet and in a bad mood, with the drizzle not letting up for a minute, Philip goaded his assistant and worked like a bull until they reached the campsite.

With empty stomachs and frayed tempers, and with the grayness of wet rocks, the campsite seemed a miserable place. That night they slept in bags that oozed water where their weight rested, bellies growling from an unimaginative meal of cold sardines and pilot biscuits. Philip dozed off, thinking of his comfortable apartment in Montreal, of his beautiful long-haired wife, and of elegant dinners with warmed plates and good wine, and in his separate tent, and somewhat oblivious to the discomforts, Tik wondered what he might have done if the accident had left him all alone in this rocky and rain-driven place.

↜ FIVE ↝

The camp was silent, a tiny huddle of tents, still as the rocks. The sun inched up over the rim of the world and hurled long shadows of hills over the water. A solitary gull hung on the wind, and the sedge cotton was brushed by faint breezes that dipped down into a hollow. A camp. A camp with no children, no dogs to rise and shake dew from their coats. A white-man camp, sad and lonely and arrogant and insolent, all at the same time.

Offshore, a kayak drifted on the green belly of the sea, coming close to a rocky islet, a skerry, nesting place of terns. The little birds began flying up with agitated cries, sounding like the grating of pebbles rubbed together. The gull, still hanging on the wind, was puzzled by this image of man and kayak, so still, looking like a fish dying at the surface. He turned in the air and swung low, wind thrumming in his wings. Then he saw it was man, and he saw, too, several nests and eggs left unprotected by the parent terns.

The man continued to stare at the sea, his vision captured

by sun on rippling water making a thousand flickering star points in his eyes.

In the bay, beluga, a dozen or more, surfaced and blew, but the man in the drifting kayak saw nothing in his dreams of no-time. . . .

By using sightings of seals as they surfaced to breathe, Philip had developed a formula for calculating the number of seals in a given area of open water. It sounded simple, but it was a rather complicated business, requiring the type of discipline and attention span which Philip felt he could not trust his assistant to maintain. He and Tik had risen early and headed their separate ways — Philip to the hill overlooking the bay, and Tik out in the kayak. Now, with a stopwatch, binoculars, hand tally, and notebook, Philip sat making timed, regular sweeps with the glasses, counting seal heads. He enjoyed being alone, and in the past weeks he had spent a lot of time doing this. Philip liked Tik, but lately the boy had been particularly irritating, stubborn and even sulky if he didn't get his own way. Only that morning, Philip had instructed Tik to take the freighter canoe and motor and go out to check the numbers of nesting eiders and other birds on a certain string of islets in Roberts Bay. Philip intended to get as many papers out of this summer trip as possible, for it was a publish-or-perish world, and besides, he liked birds. So for two weeks Tik had been carrying out nest and egg counts, observing the numbers of eggs destroyed by gulls, the distances between nests, and a dozen other things. The boy did that kind of work well, and it kept him out of the way. That morning, Tik had argued, as he always did, that he wanted to go in the kayak. He finally won by smugly pointing out that the noise of the outboard would disturb the seals as well as the nesting birds. It was true, so Philip had let him go in the kayak, irritated that he had given in, and even more irritated by the thought that it would take Tik an extra three hours to do the job and get back to camp, where there were many chores to do — seal skulls to be cleaned, measured, labeled and packed, and a couple of hundred seal jaws from which teeth must be extracted for aging. The local Inuit hunters brought the jaws in, and Philip paid them.

Earlier in the morning, while counting seals, Philip had watched Tik make use of ebb current, which carried water from deep bays and convoluted inlets, traveling easily and swiftly out to the islets, two or three miles distant. He had watched Tik's tiny figure and the flocks of ducks, mere specks at this distance, that rose up at his intrusion. Philip noted at that time that the boy was working quickly, causing minimal disturbance, for Philip had always stressed that the birds must be allowed to get back to their nests before the marauding bandit gulls took their toll of eggs and ducklings. Having checked, and seen that things were going well, Philip went back to his own surveys, looking forward to Tik's getting back to camp and cooking up a meal. The boy's cooking was improving.

He swept the area with binoculars again, counting three dots. He noted the time it took to do the sweep, the light and cloud conditions, the sea's state. He had to be careful that those were really seals and not just ducks or other birds on the water. The wind seemed to be freshening, and this would make counting more difficult, with different factors affecting the formula. It was just about slack water. The boy had been out for hours, and it was time he was heading back, making use of the currents. Philip searched the area and saw that the kayak was just drifting. Hell and damnation, the bloody boy was daydreaming again!

The last island that Tik had surveyed was one of a string of bare, rocky skerries that extended north and south down the bay. This islet was only a hundred yards long and forty wide, with little beaches deep in broken shells of mollusks, white, mother of pearl, metallic blue. Vegetation was sparse, just a few clumps of coarse grass, in and around which the eider nests crowded, two or three feet apart, with gull nests scattered in among them. As Tik had approached, alarmed ducks had flown up, many of them fouling their nests as they did so — a protective habit that perhaps dissuaded some of the fussier predators. However, nothing puts a gull off its food. The ducks landed in the water a few yards offshore, or joined other groups flying around, many skimming close to Tik as he picked his way carefully, counting the olive green eggs in their soft, warm beds of brownish gray down. Once in a while he checked an egg, putting it close to his ear to detect movement or clicking before putting it carefully back and covering the clutch over with down, as a female eider would do if she left the nest when not in a panic.

He finished his survey of this last islet and washed his hands in seawater, then pushed off and drifted in the kayak so as to watch the birds return to their nests, and to see how often gulls got to the nests first. The current carried him past another, smaller island, home of terns, and they came out in squadrons to chitter and attack, hovering and diving. Tik watched fascinated at the patterns of the terns' wings against the sky, and shifted his gaze down as they dove at him, pecking lightly at his head. The kayak drifted. The sea, rippled by breezes, reflected sun, and soon Tik was held by a myriad glittering lights bombarding his retina. Time stopped. . . .

Philip spotted a pod of beluga in the bay, and at the same time he spotted the Peterhead boat making its slow, chugging process in his direction. Then the boat veered in the direction of the beluga, and Philip wondered if such a boat were fast enough to hunt the little white whales. But then, when the pod turned and headed east, the Peterhead stayed on its new course, not going after the whales at all, but heading in the direction of the slowly drifting kayak.

The sound of the boat engine did not intrude upon Tik's dream, and he did not come out of it until the Peterhead came alongside and the bow wave began to rock his kayak violently. Strong brown hands reached down to him, and laughing greetings were exchanged as they pulled him aboard. The kayak was hoisted up and lashed to the gunwales of the sturdy wooden vessel.

"Ooniak! Ipeelee! Tommy! Now a man is joyous to see you!" Tik turned to Neviaksi, Ipeelee's younger brother, who was at the boat's tiller. "This one sees you also, Neviaksi."

Neviaksi smiled and noted the look of admiration the young white man showed for Neviaksi's eider-skin parka. He seemed so open, this one, like a big, muscular child.

Ooniak, Tommy and Ipeelee were all delighted to see the young man, and amused to find him offshore, dreaming and drifting on the sea. Patiently, and with quiet dignity, they answered the barrage of his disjointed and ungrammatical questions. They had arrived the day before. Ooniak's wife and young Annie were now at Neviaksi's camp. Tommy nudged Tik in the ribs, asking if he was going to get in his kayak and paddle over to Neviaksi's tent to see Annie, to take her some tea and sugar. They all laughed at Tik's embarrassment, and it was this very embarrassment that endeared him to Ipeelee even more. Ooniak had brought mail from the settlement. Yes, they could stay a little for some tea and sweet biscuits. They were going north on a walrus hunt, and on hearing this, Tik yearned to go with them.

Philip had reached the camp ahead of them, and from the shore he watched the boat come into the inlet and drop anchor. Apart from Tik's kayak, two sealskin kayaks were also lashed to the Peterhead, and a freighter canoe was towed behind. They launched Tik's little craft, then the four Inuit followed in the big canoe. Once ashore, they shook hands with Philip and handed him the mail, while Tik went into the big tent to put a kettle on.

While they were drinking tea, to Tik's surprise and delight, Philip asked if one of the Inuit would stay behind, offering them ten dollars a day, food, and the skins of the seals they would hunt. Philip said he could provide ammunition and a rifle, for he had brought with him a fine, high-powered .270, as well as the twelve-gauge shotgun and the .22 that Tik liked to use. He also had the eighteen-foot freighter canoe, motor and gasoline. In those times, Philip's offer was generous indeed.

The four hunters talked among themselves, but it was Ipeelee who made the decision. The Peterhead was the joint property of Ooniak and Ipeelee, but Ooniak was its captain, for he best understood the engine and the sails. Tommy was one of the finest harpooners and rifle shots in the country, and Neviaksi, Ipeelee's youngest brother, knew the ice conditions, the anchorages, the vagaries of current and wind, and the best places to find walrus. It was he, old Ipeelee, who would accept this easy task of hunting seal, for which he would receive dollars as well as skins. He had grown ancient and weary, and for an old man, aiee, it would be easy and profitable, and besides, they needed dollars to pay for the gasoline that the engine on the boat drank as a hunter drinks tea. There could be no doubt as to who should stay. Ooniak bowed to his father's decision, knowing full well how much the old man loved to hunt walrus, and of how each of his father's decisions were made for the sake of others.

"Father, we will hunt walrus for two weeks and then return for you before you grow too fat on the bannock and butter of the white man. As we approached, we saw many beluga, and it would be good if we hunted them and took back *muktuk* as well as the meat and hides and ivory of walrus. No man knows the whales as does Ipeelee, and you can teach us the best ways to catch them."

"Yes, truly," said Neviaksi. "Foolish hunters may miss the walrus, and then we will need my brother's skill to enable us to return with joy to our families."

"Indeed," said Tommy, the youngest of them, "and with the dollars, you can buy a radio, and we can dance in our camp."

Ipeelee then explained to Tik what they had decided, and Tik told Philip. Philip had hoped for one of the younger hunters, but he did not show his disappointment; the old fellow was no doubt pretty knowledgeable about seals, and good in a boat. He shook hands with Ipeelee and passed around his tobacco pouch. At least, thought Philip, the old fellow would be less reckless in the freighter canoe than Tik.

"I suppose we'll have to clear out the work benches and put the old boy in here," said Philip.

"Oh, no," said Tik, "he can sleep in the spare tent, with me. There's room for two."

"Well, if he doesn't mind, I guess that's good enough." Tik took Ipeelee to show him their tent, and Ipeelee smiled and said good, good, amused that the young white man should be worried that he, Ipeelee, who had slept hundreds of nights in the snow with his dogs, would approve of the sleeping place. He nudged the young man in the ribs.

"A man should bring women from Neviaksi's camp to warm our tent," he said, and then all four Inuit guffawed with amusement at how easily Tik turned red. Neviaksi said that they would bring back the largest penis bone from the strongest of the walrus bulls, and get the "doctor" (meaning Philip) to graft it onto the old man, for without such an aid it would do no good to bring women into the camp anyway. The good natured banter went on until it came time for the three hunters to offload Ipeelee's rifle and sleeping robes and his small skin bag of possessions, and for them all to exchange good wishes for the hunting to come.

Tik, who got himself out of bed each morning with the aid of an alarm clock, was just a little upset that Ipeelee had risen before him and had gone out. Tik had hoped to please the old man by preparing a hot breakfast and having it ready for him when he got out of bed. Philip placed great store in such luxuries. But that morning it had been especially difficult for Tik to get up, Ipeelee snored thunderously, keeping Tik awake. He crawled out of his sleeping bag, dressed, dragged on his boots, and went outside to urinate, then to brush his teeth and splash cold water on his face from a nearby stream. He had got the stove going, and the porridge and tea made, when Ipeelee returned to camp, carrying his old brass telescope under his arm.

"Ice moves in the bay, but not much. It will be a good day for seals. Water will be calm, and ice will hide the canoe. It is a good day."

Tik was delighted, and hurried through his breakfast, finishing it before Philip got out of bed. He readied the canoe, filling the gas tank and the spare drum with mixed oil and fuel. He placed one of their two harpoons, a gaff, and a sort of sinking grapnel made of four large shark hooks set in lead with a line attached. He shifted the canoe down rollers and into the water, and tied a wooden box amidships. The box contained sample jars, test tubes, preservative, waterproof labels, dissecting instruments, tape measures, a heavy brass hanging scale, and various other paraphernalia used for taking samples and data from the seals they killed. Tik was neatly coiling a harpoon line when Philip came down.

"What do you think you're doing?" He was always bad tempered in the morning.

"I got the canoe ready to go. Ipeelee says it's a good day for seals."

"Who said we were going after seals?"

"Nobody, but Ipeelee said that ice was coming in, and bringing seals, and that the water was good and smooth for hunting."

"Well, Ipeelee is not the boss around here," said Philip testily. "I'm the one who decides what is to be done, and if I decide to go hunting, I'll tell you. As it happens, I have a lot to do around camp, and so do you." He turned his back and went into the big tent, where his breakfast had been kept hot for him. Tik was furious. This was the North! A man hunted when he could, when conditions were good to hunt! He wanted to shout at Philip, but knew he dared not.

They did eventually go hunting. It was too good a day to miss, but it seemed to Tik that Philip puttered around camp until past ten in the morning just to prove a point.

Ipeelee took the bow position, and Philip the tiller of the outboard, with Tik sitting amidships. They were not out long when Philip spotted a seal. He turned the bow around and Ipeelee got off a quick shot with Tik's .22, creasing the animal's skull and stunning it slightly. It was about to dive when they got close enough for the Inuit to hurl the harpoon, securing it. He and Tik pulled the animal into the canoe and laid it on a thwart, its bullet-creased skull resting on the gunwales while the animal was giving up its ghost and returning blood to the sea. Ipeelee began explaining, in simple and slowly spoken words, the water ritual, telling Tik that the seal spirit should have fresh water, for which it craved during its life in the salty seas. He explained that without proper respect and the gift of water, the seal spirit would perhaps not return in seal form, and could even affect a stupid hunter in terrible ways, or worse still, cause the Sea Mother, she who was sometimes called Anarquagssaq, sometimes Luma, sometimes other names, to be angry. It was terrible, reflected the old man as he cut out the harpoon barb and recoiled the line, that young Inuit neglected these important things, and for this reason, the seals were becoming scarcer.

"What is he talking about?" asked Philip.

"He's telling me about old hunting rituals, and the goddess of the sea," said Tik.

"Well, kill that poor bloody seal," said Philip, anguished by the sight of blood streaming from the dying animal's mouth and nostril, trailing scarlet in the water beside the canoe. As if understanding, although Ipeelee spoke no English, he stayed Tik's hand.

"Leave him be, it is almost over. His soul prepares to return, and now the seal sees dreams. This hunter would not disturb the dreams. The seal feels no pain. His body does not move in pain. Leave him." But Philip did not understand the old man's words and could stand the sight no longer. He left his place at the stern of the canoe and came to smash his big fist down on the seal's head, crushing the fragile yearling skull and bursting both eyes out of it in a porridge of brains and blood, gray and red.

This unneedfully violent act startled the Inuit, who had seen the quietness of death, with pain arrested by shock, coming over the animal. He could not understand this act, like the act of a madman crazy to kill, and anything he could not understand, Ipeelee was wary of. Tik too was startled, and now, looking at this mess of the once sleek head, he suddenly retched, and leaned over the side of the canoe and vomited.

"You big baby!" cried Philip derisively. "Think yourself a tough hunter, do you? Can't even finish off an animal when it's dying." Embarrassed beyond words, Tik wiped his face and sat hunched up and still, saying nothing, while Ipeelee, now even more puzzled by the meaning of the vomiting, thought about the possible reasons behind it. Perhaps it was that this one, Tikkisi, was atoning for the violence by giving up food from his own stomach to the sea? There could surely be no other reason, for they had none of them eaten rotten meat, nor had they eaten too much. Aieee, the white men were strange, he thought, but the young one was easier to be with than the one they called Nanook. A man would have to be careful not to offend that one. A man would have to make a spell of protection for himself, yes indeed.

Despite the fact that it was an excellent day for hunting, just as Ipeelee would have predicted, they took no more seals that day.

Later, after returning to camp, Ipeelee sat on a box down by the shore and thought about things, humming a tune, enjoying the warmth of the sun, and bringing out an unfinished carving of a bearded seal. Tik was boiling seal jaws in order to loosen teeth for easier extraction. He would pull them out, preserve them in glycerine and alcohol, and later, in the laboratory, the teeth would be cut and ground into thin slices and examined under a microscope. This would enable Philip to count growth rings and come up with an estimate of the animal's age. As he worked, Tik listened to the old man's humming and tried to figure out where he had heard the tune before, until he realized that it was a hymn. They had finished lunch, and despite his earlier sickness, Tik ate ravenously, aware that the old Inuit was watching him very carefully.

Philip came down and put the .270 and a small haversack into the canoe. He had his binoculars around his neck.

"Shall we go hunting, Ipeelee?"

Ipeelee got up at the sound of his name and, eagerly, Tik jumped up too, turning off the stove and the pot of steaming, stinking seal jaws.

"You've had enough hunting for today, Tik," Philip said, "and anyway, I want you to get those jaws finished today." He saw the look of angry disappointment and added, "Don't sulk."

"I'm not sulking!" Tik snapped, glaring now at the bigger man. Ipeelee watched the two white men and recalled that once before he had seen such an undercurrent of bad feeling build up between two hunters who, like these two, had kept it hidden until one day when they were building a snow house, one of the hunters had stretched to lift a snow block, exposing his naked belly under the parka. The sight had been too much for his companion, who had pierced the man through the entrails with a snow knife, and then run away, frightened by his own actions. Philip launched the canoe off the sloping beach and held it for Ipeelee to scramble aboard.

"Seriously, Tik, I do want you to finish those jaws," said Philip, and just before he hopped into the canoe he added, almost as an afterthought, "We don't really need three people, it's too many for this canoe."

"Yeah, that's OK." Tik waded into the water as far as his boots would let him and lifted the bow over a rock. He gave it a shove at the bow that made Philip stumble, sending it well clear of the submerged rocks close into shore. Philip began to say something angrily, but Ipeelee started the motor and waved to Tik before turning the canoe around and heading out of the inlet and into the bay.

Tik hurried and finished the unpleasant, smelly job quicker than usual. He took his .22 and a box of fifty rounds, and took also the second harpoon and line and attached the line to a round, brilliant orange rubber float, a modification that Philip had dreamt up to replace the traditional sealskin floats of the Inuit hunters. Tik had stitched thongs to his kayak to take harpoon and killing lance, with a little flat box lashed behind the seat to hold a coiled harpoon line. The float too was secured to the kayak, in such a way that it would not fall off, but would come loose with the least tug of the line. Tik was excited almost to the point of carelessness, and he had to force himself to slow down, to ritualize every last check of weapons and equipment. Without really thinking about why he did it, he went over to where Ipeelee had been sitting and picked up the unfinished carving. It had seal form, and the head and whiskers were clearly defined. Only the back flippers and the final polishing had to be done. In Tik's hands, the stone felt alive, for it was warm with sun, as the dark stone had absorbed energy where it had lain. As he stroked the carving, it seemed as if he could almost feel the smoothness of seal hair beneath his fingers. He wrapped it carefully in a piece of cloth and put it into the front pocket of his anorak. Ipeelee wouldn't mind, he knew, and the carving might bring him luck.

Once out of the mouth of the inlet, where the ebb tide caused long streamers of kelp to flow in undulating motions, traveling, speeding, yet going nowhere, Tik was in a world of water, sky and ice. It was calm, and he could see down to the rocks as they descended into gloom some thirty or forty feet below. Jellyfish, some just hanging, and some pulsating forward and upward, were scattered all over, and Tik watched them, seeing in them worlds of unimaginable antiquity. The submerged portions of floating ice loomed huge and water-smoothed, and Tik edged his way out among and over, out through the leads, until he was surrounded by ice, and it was as if the water floated on ice, and he and his kayak might be swallowed up in the whiteness. In places, floes crowded together, leaving only narrow, high-walled channels, with pinnacles, buttresses, arches, and all the shapes of classical architecture as well as the fluid shapes of modern sculpture. Ledges of ice, blue white, constantly dripping, leaned out over the water, sometimes giving way with booming cracks, smashing into the sea and shoving miniature tidal waves here and there, rocking the kayak and bobbing smaller pieces of ice like apples in a tub. And all the time, the ice was moving, acres of broken floes and small bergs coming into the bay with the pressure of more ice and water outside, all the while turning with the tidal currents, piling up against headlands, cracking, straining, crunching. Some floes, having lost top weight when a piece fell off, would suddenly shift position in the water, causing submerged portions to rise up out of the sea like angry monsters.

Tik moved quietly through the channels, following the sound of a loon's cry, feeling again this illogical and irrational desire to kill the bird, hold it to him, know in closeness the origins of that wonderful, wild sound.

He rounded a bend in a channel, thinking to see the loon, but instead he heard a snorting exhalation of breath, and there, not fifteen yards away, was the head of a big, bearded seal! Already the kayak was gliding toward the animal, and Tik could clearly see its body under the surface of the water, silhouetted against the blue white foot of a slab of floe. The seal seemed breathless, terrified of something, and it did not perceive the quiet ripple of water against the kayak's hull. Tik shipped the paddle and took up the harpoon in his right hand, the line in his left. Closer, closer he glided until the bow of the kayak was within two yards of the seal. Too late, the seal knew the danger from behind, and with a furious thrashing of its hind flippers, it turned its body to dive. But when the bearded seal dives, it rolls its body partway out of the water, and by this time Tik had hurled his harpoon with all his strength, body braced, stomach and chest muscles contracting forcefully, air exploding from his lungs.

The harpoon struck and the line whipped away so fast that Tik was startled into snatching at his paddle, thinking that the float might not let go, and that the little craft might tip over. But the orange float skimmed across the surface and then dipped under as the line became taut, and the barb and the tail of the harpoon head were pulled parallel to the entry wound. The separated haft came clear but remained attached by a loop of thong to the line. The seal was trying to head for another patch of open water, a hundred fifty yards away, but the drag of the float was too much, and the seal turned back. As the seal surfaced, a .22 shot creased the top of his skull and whined away over the ice. He dove again, and again he spent himself trying to pull down the buoyant orange ball. This time Tik took aim more carefully, bracing his elbow, waiting, ready to fire as soon as the seal should surface again. From a distance of forty yards, the .22 bullet struck the seal in the head, smashing an ear bone but not killing him. The seal's agony became Tik's remorse, and he waited again for the seal to reappear. Its dives were becoming shorter now. The orange float moved erratically from one side of the lead to another, and Tik followed it, trying to guess where the animal would come up. The next shot must kill!

With an explosive rush of air and a swirl of sound, something erupted from the water behind Tik. He thrust the rifle into its case and spun the kayak around, bewildered and a little frightened now, seeing the vast, sleek, black and white form pass directly beneath the kayak with an awesome speed and beauty. Yards away, the mortally wounded seal surfaced again, confronted now with death in two shapes: the surface thing with its barbs and bangs and stings, and the great jaws of the killer whale.

It was from the killer whales that this seal had been escaping in the first place, diving from open patch to lead, hoping to evade its pursuers with their shrill underwater hunting calls. But now the biggest of the pack of six had followed him right under the ice to this small lead, which was only fifty yards wide, yet still wide enough for these athletes of the ocean to turn and charge. Motionless with shocked surprise, Tik watched the whale speed toward the wounded seal, only to turn at the last moment to surface with another blast of air. The black fin, triangular, six feet high and slightly floppy at the tip, knifed through the water like a sail. He was at least twenty-five feet long, maybe more, and the water magnified him. With curiosity, the big, bull, pack leader nosed the orange float, then took it in his mouth, pulling it for a yard or so, very gently taking up the slack in the line. Then he let it go and turned again, rolling his body so that one eye came out of the water, examining with frank curiosity the man in the kayak. The smell of the whale's breath washed over Tik, who thought that the whale would surely take "his" seal, and for several minutes the huge animal cruised between the float, the dying seal, and the kayak, and Tik wondered if the whale was making a decision, or simply observing this phenomenon.

This particular hunting pack had cruised the edge of the ice mass, having finished a wide sweep along the coast. Already they had taken several immature ringed seals, while the other, older and experienced seals had fled into places in the ice where the whales could not follow. At this moment the other five were on the other side of the floe, listening to the high-pitched sounds of their leader, chasing a few other seals who frantically sought refuge in the pack ice. Just when it seemed inevitable to Tik that the killer whale would make off with his harpooned seal, yet another head popped up, a hundred yards from them both. Giving no time for thought, Tik brought up his rifle and fired, and although a hundred yards is a pretty fair range for seal with a .22, the bullet took the little yearling through the eye and killed it instantly. Swift as an arrow, the killer whale came to a decision and sped underwater to where the second seal floated, bleeding, head down. So sudden was his departure that the swirl of water caused by his flukes spun the kayak around, and Tik had to grab for the paddle to steady it. The whale took the second seal and was gone, under the jammed floes to open water on the other side.

From the floe edge, where he and Philip had been watching breathlessly, Ipeelee lowered the rifle and let out a long cry of surprise and wonder, and of relief too, for he had not wanted to shoot at the great sea brother with this rifle. Philip, running with great bounding strides, reached the lead first.

"Tik! The float! Bring the float over here!"

When the killer whales had come close to the freighter canoe, Ipeelee had insisted that they take it out of the water and onto the ice. The old Inuit held the swift black and white hunters of the oceans in almost superstitious dread. Having gotten the canoe up onto a flat and level floe, Philip had been astounded to see what appeared to be a tall, triangular fin cruising through ice. They went closer, with Philip excited at the chance of seeing a big bull killer whale at close quarters. It was then that they had come upon the drama enacted between Tik, the harpooned seal, and the small seal sacrifice.

Tik passed the float and line to Philip, and Ipeelee steadied the kayak for him so that he could get out and haul it up.

"My god, I was scared for a minute that he was going to take you," said Philip.

Remembering the curious intelligence of the whale's scrutiny, Tik shook his head. "I don't think so, Phil. He was pretty interested in my seal though. I guess he must have been chasing it when I stuck it with my harpoon." Ipeelee called to them and pointed. The pod of killer whales, now rejoined by their senior member, was heading back toward the mouth of the bay.

Ipeelee cut a slit in the lower jaw and threaded a line through it so that they could haul it head first and thus make use of the natural streamlining of the seal's body and the lie of its fur when they hauled its four-hundred-pound bulk up onto the ice. Philip and Tik took measurements of length, girth, blubber thickness and so forth and then waited for Ipeelee to skin the animal in such a way that its incredibly tough hide could be used to make harpoon lines or dog traces. The job was done quickly, and soon the hide and thick blubber lay alongside the carcass in heavy, floppy rings about two feet wide. Philip put away his camera and got ready to collect the internal tissue samples that he needed. Tik struck off the lower jaw for later extraction of teeth. As soon as Philip's knife penetrated the body cavity of the seal, blood came out in congealing blobs onto the ice. Ipeelee pointed.

"The harpoon struck deep and true, Tikkisi. You are a good hunter."

It was true that the harpoon had hit deep, and it was the harpoon and not the bullets that had killed the animal. It had entered at an angle under the seal's ribs, piercing skin, blubber and flesh to lodge and tear at the tough muscle of the diaphragm. A truly powerful throw.

Pride and sadness welled up within the young man as he gazed down at the pitifully bloodied form. Ipeelee looked on him with pleasure, for it was a valuable animal, and killed in the old way. How he would enjoy berating those idle young men in the settlement, telling them how a *Kabluna* had killed such a seal with a harpoon, from a kayak! Aieeee! But none of them would believe the circumstances!

They finished butchering the seal and then loaded the heavy chunks of blubber and flesh, and the valuable rings of hide and blubber, into the canoe. Already the gulls gathered at impatient distances to pick at the remains. Five other seals, all of the smaller but tastier ringed variety, lay covered by a canvas in the bottom of the canoe. By this time the gunwales were barely above the water.

"Seal liver and onions for supper tonight, Tik," said Philip, his grin hiding the concern he felt for the overloaded condition of the canoe. Tik grinned back and rubbed his stomach, making faces.

In camp, while they did their data collection on the five ringed seals, and while Ipeelee skinned them, Philip spoke what was on his mind.

"All things considered, I'm pleased with the seals we got, especially yours. Nevertheless, I'm going to forbid you to go out in the kayak by yourself. It's dangerous, and you have no real sense of danger."

"But Phil!" Tik put down his own knife. "You told me yourself that there is no real evidence of killer whales' harming humans!"

"It's not just the whales, it's all kinds of things. I know you're very good in the kayak, and I know I've been letting you go out alone to the eider islands, but this latest business has been making me think. It's just too risky. You can go along the coast, as long as you keep within a hundred yards of shore, and you can go around the inlet, but not out into the bay. That's final."

Glum and silent, Tik went on cutting and measuring. There

was no use in arguing, for when Philip said something, he usually meant it. But for Tik, no experience was as fulfilling as the solitary hunt. In the kayak he could move silently, close to the water, and he became aware of things around, above, and even below him. The thin hull of the kayak seemed to transmit to him the very essence of the undersea world, vibrations and other energies, and as he brooded about this he wondered, "Did I really hear the cries of the whales? Thin and muffled, perhaps, but there?" Or had it been just a loose strut creaking under his body weight? He resolved to ask Ipeelee about it, for he would know, and in thinking about this, he gradually pushed the gloom out of his mind.

In the mind of the old Inuit there was no doubt that this strange boy-man had powerful affiliations with the sea creatures. When Tik shyly produced Ipeelee's unfinished carving, still warm from his pocket, and returned it to him, Ipeelee decided that he must finish the carving and keep it in a special place, not to sell it in the winter at the trading post. This carving brought good luck, it had been recognized by a latent or "sleeping" shaman, a shaman who did not know himself, a shaman still enveloped in worldly things, encased in the womb of childhood. Ah, if only he had been Inuit! It was indeed puzzling! The boy did not observe proper forms. Despite being told, he had forgotten to give the seal he killed a drink of fresh water, and it was he, old Ipeelee, who had melted snow in his mouth and spat it into the mouth of the dead seal. And yet, when the killer whale was disputing with the white man as to who should take the seal, and after all, the whale had every right to take that one, for it was he who had chased him into the lead, calling to him under the silver roof of the open waters and in the undersea chambers of ice and echoes — yes indeed, the whale truly had a right — yet the boy-man had had the power to bring up another seal, and had killed it with a skillful shot! How else but through strong powers could even a young and foolish seal be brought into the presence of a big bull killer whale? How else but through strong powers could a mere boy end a dispute so skillfully? Truly, the more a man observed life, the more wonderful it was. An old man would have to give these happenings much thought.

In the next couple of days, onshore winds brought in so much ice that hunting became impossible. Accordingly, Ipeelee walked overland to Neviaksi's camp, from which Noah, Joe and Danny were still hoping to gather a good stock of seal skins for trade later in the season. In his dreams, Ipeelee had seen that the hunting at Neviaksi's camp had not been good for a few days, while Philip's camp was so overloaded with meat that they could not use it or even cut it into strips to dry. Ipeelee was anxious to share this bounty with the other people, and perhaps, if he could admit it to himself, he was anxious to regale them with stories of what he had been seeing.

As he walked over the tundra with the cries of birds in his ears, and the mosquitoes kept down by wind that made the fragile yellow poppies bow and dance at his feet, Ipeelee sang a special song to help himself think. He thought about Tikkisi, Boy-who-smiles, who was forever asking questions like a child eagerly gathering berries in an open pail, and he thought too of the other one, and of his disconcerting habit of putting everything into little books, as if he were locking up the *sila*, the soul-essence of life, between covers. He thought too of the bad air that grew between the two white men, and the lack of real understanding that the older man had of the changes that were coming over Tikkisi, and of the dangers of these. Then he thought about his granddaughter Annie and wished again that Tikkisi was Inuit, for his not being so would, or could, bring much pain to her. But first, thought Ipeelee, there were things which the man called Nanook must be made to understand, and to do this Ipeelee would speak to the white man at Neviaksi's camp, the one they called Caleedee, who spoke the language of the Inuit well. Yes, that was the best thing to do.

⤙ SIX ⤚

Ipeelee, Noah, Joe and Clyde came back overland from Neviaksi's camp in order to carry back loads of meat. Under large rocks, close by the shore, they cached the blubber, now gone butter yellow in the sun, to store it for a time suitable for moving it by sea. Before heading back with his seventy-pound load of meat, Clyde asked Philip if he could speak with him. They walked together up a ridge and sat down, close by one of the ancient stone navigation markers of the Inuit. Philip passed over his tobacco pouch.

"Look, Phil," said Clyde, getting straight to the point, "you once told me to mind my own business with regard to you and Tik, right?" Philip began to say something but Clyde held up his hand.

"Well, Ipeelee has asked me to talk with you about Tik, so just try to listen and understand. OK?"

"Certainly, Clyde, and to get the record straight, I'm sorry about what happened in the canoe, and I don't mind your saying anything. It's just that I've known Tik since he was fourteen and I know him to be a good lad, the best, but he can get pretty difficult to handle. You are on the outside, and you don't see it. He's big, powerful, intelligent, but still just a kid. You know, he's barely turned nineteen, and in many ways, he's still immature." Philip lit his pipe, squinting at Clyde through the puffs of smoke as the yellow flame of the match bobbed up and down.

"Sure, I know, but on the other hand, he has made a very favorable impression with the Eskimos, and they often see things we don't. Anyway, I'll try to convey to you what Ipeelee has told me. Don't laugh though, because I think it's serious."

"Go ahead, I'm listening."

"Well," began Clyde, "I think I got it all straight, but some of it may be garbled, because their language is complex, to say the least, and they have such a wealth of words about anything, well, shall we say, metaphysical." Philip arched his eyebrows but said nothing, and Clyde took a puff on his pipe. "Ipeelee believes that Tik has a supernatural attachment to the creatures of the sea, and he believes that this attachment might be physically dangerous for him. It seems that when Ooniak brought the Peterhead around, they got right up alongside Tik before he was aware of them, and you know what a row that engine makes. Ipeelee says that Tik was in a trance."

Philip interrupted him. "Hell, Tik is forever daydreaming!" Why, he thought, Tik had been like that in class, and he recalled summer afternoons in England, the image of Tik sitting at his desk in the biology lab, staring out of the window, gazing at a sparrow or a cloud or nothing at all, while the other students scribbled furiously in the notebooks or bent over their dissections.

"Wait on, now, this wasn't just ordinary daydreaming.

Ipeelee interprets it as Tik's spirit being in tune with the sea, so that the sea is able to call him, causing him to go into the trance. Ipeelee has seen this before, and says that with certain men of this nature there is a danger of their going out in the calmest of conditions and never coming back. Such men would paradoxically be safe in rough water. Tik is a rough-water kayaker, sure enough, we know that. Ipeelee also says that there is no danger if another hunter is nearby, because others can recognize the trance and bring him out of it."

"How?"

"Ipeelee says that the easiest way is to pass in front, or shake or bump the kayak. You see, according to Ipeelee, the sea creatures call to those hunters they love, and once this dream or trance is induced, the hunter loses fear of the water and drowns, or as Ipeelee puts it, 'is carried into the deep places of the sea.' " Clyde paused to see if Philip was being scornful in his cynical British way, but Philip looked interested.

"You know, Phil, I have read of similar things among the Greenlanders, the best kayak men of all. When they hunt on days when there is a slight ripple on the water, they take care of each other, hunt in pairs or more. They say that the glittering light off the water can mesmerize a man. Another man can break it by giving the kayak a jerk. When you really think of it, it's not that farfetched either, and I reckon that the Eskimo explanation of the phenomenon is as good as ours. Ever heard of a stroboscopic trance?"

"Good lord! So that's it!" said Philip. "The flickering light of sun on water induces a stroboscopic trance!"

"Yes, flashing lights, frequency coinciding with the frequency of the subject's alpha waves. Makes you think, eh?"

"Indeed, and if I remember it rightly, some people can go

into a trance, or into a deep trance, more easily than others. You know, if Ipeelee is right about Tik, that demonstrates amazing perception."

"Well, there you go. You see, don't you, that the hunting Eskimos are extremely perceptive. The crux of this conversation is, though, that Ipeelee urges you to watch Tik carefully if he goes out on calm days in the kayak. He knows how much the kid likes to go out and hunt. Tik fancies himself an old-style kayak man, and he really doesn't have the experience yet. Who knows, maybe he is a favorite of the Eskimo Poseidon?"

"I appreciate you telling me all this, Clyde, and thank Ipeelee for me. He's an impressive old man."

"Damn right he is, more than you know. You realize that he was born on these islands? They weren't known to whites until the 1930s, which means that old Ipeelee, for more than thirty years of his life, lived the ways of prehistoric Eskimos. Neviaksi, Noah, Joe, Danny — they're all a bit scared of him, you know."

"Really? Why? He seems to be a harmless old man."

"Yeah, well, they say he's an *angakok*."

"What's that?"

"A magician, a shaman." Clyde got to his feet and knocked out his pipe. "I'd better be going."

"Why don't you stay the night?"

"No, they want to get back with the meat. By the way, I'm writing up notes on some of this, and I'd like to know your version of what happened the other day, you know, between the seals and the killer whale."

As an anthropologist, Clyde was interested in the differing realities of white and Inuit observations. As they walked down the ridge, Philip told the story as he had seen it, if anything playing down Tik's hunting skill.

"You know what Ipeelee says?" said Clyde. "He says that Tik took a carving of a bearded seal, recognizing that Ipeelee must have put some power into the carving. Without knowing it, Tik was calling to the sea creatures to help him. The whales answered, and brought him a bearded seal, which Tik harpooned. Then the chief whale, hearing the cries of the dying seal, came to ask for a present in return, or else he would take the seal himself, because the sea creatures don't usually help white men. So Tik called up another seal and gave it to the whale. I reckon that story is just as good as yours. You know what? I've heard Ipeelee tell that story several times, and each time he subtly attached more meaning to it, so that all the people who hear it believe it implicitly. You couldn't disprove any of it."

Philip laughed. "Would you like Tik to make stories for you? That Celtic imagination of his should come up with some dandies."

"No doubt. Oh, there's another thing, Phil — I've decided to get Ooniak to take me up to one of the northern camps again after he finishes his whale hunt here. They're going to be back in a couple of weeks, I should guess. I'm going to be pretty busy, so this might be the last time we run into each other until the end of summer."

The ten days that followed were filled with successful hunts, and they took another forty seals. Every second day, Ipeelee and Tik made a trip to Neviaksi's camp, carrying meat and blubber, and skins to be scraped, stretched, and cured by the camp women. Annie was always there, but the two young people spoke little to each other, only glanced shyly, and smiled, and Tik thought about her a lot, though he never had a chance to be alone with her. Annie seemed to him like a tundra flower, delicate in her beauty, an attractiveness easily passed by or missed, yet with roots that ran tough and deep, and hard to touch. Sometimes, when he was alone, he had imaginary conversations with her, and touched her body with his thoughts.

Ipeelee spent as much time as he could with Tik, although Philip was very demanding of both of their services. He showed Tik how to make fox traps from rocks, how to throw a harpoon with accuracy and ease, how to make fish weirs from walls of stones, how to find grasses and roots to eat, how to find small delicacies such as edible seaweeds along the tide line, how to do a hundred little things about the land. After they had finished their work, the young man and the old Inuit would walk together, or sometimes they would play the harpoon and float game, laughing like small boys. Under Ipeelee's instruction, Tik's cast of the harpoon improved immensely, and he realized what a lucky fluke it was for him to have taken that first seal. Ipeelee, in turn, appreciated the way the boy could handle his kayak, and admired the craft too, although it took him some time to get used to the feathered paddles.

Each day that Philip took Ipeelee out in the motor-driven canoe to hunt, Tik felt resentful that he should not be allowed to go out and hunt too. However, he had plenty to do, and the days passed quickly enough. The evenings were pleasant, with Ipeelee endeavoring to pass as much information and knowledge to the young man as possible in the short time available. He firmly believed that a time would come again when only knowledge of the old skills would enable men to survive in the north country, and he wished to impart as much as he could to anyone who might be able to keep it. Ah, but so much had been lost already!

Philip's feelings about Ipeelee's attentions to Tik were complicated. On the one hand he felt gratified that his assistant-pupil should be thought so highly of by the old Eskimo, and on the other hand he felt excluded, and with exclusion he felt jealousy, a jealousy which made him despise himself for his own pettiness. But it was there, and it was there because Tik seemed to have found a new hero. Silly little quarrels sprang up between them, nonsensical things that caused them both to feel extreme anger and momentary dislike of each other. Tik forgot to fill the lamp. Philip threw out a pot of warm water that Tik had wanted to wash dishes with. Tik put a pot of jam on the table at breakfast instead of a pot of marmalade. Philip got up late for breakfast and then complained that the porridge was cold. Stupid things, all of them, things without meaning except that they hid other, unspoken conflicts. It was obvious to Philip that Tik no longer performed tasks for him happily and willingly, but regarded them as chores, to be done and finished with. This was no longer the eager boy of the previous expedition, who had hung on Philip's every word and had gone around camp trying to find things to do that would please him. This Tik was three inches taller, twenty pounds heavier, deeper voiced, distant, often strange, often resentful, speaking more and more around camp, in Philip's presence, in that terribly difficult and complicated language of the Eskimos. Philip, in his turn, became distant too, spending more and more time alone in his tent with his notes, his drawings and his thoughts.

In reality, Tik did not comprehend what had happened between them either, and there were times when he too chose to be alone, to walk over the tundra, hear the cry of wildfowl, and to lie on the ground, burying his face in the moss and lichens, filling his nostrils and lungs with the smell of the earth. He wanted to get away from the turmoil within himself and it was at these times that he wanted to be close to the land, to feel it through the soles of his sealskin boots, or in his nostrils. He wanted to come as close to the land as he came to the sea when he moved in the kayak, feeling the water rippling and pressing against his buttocks through the flexible hull. Life was thrusting itself upon him with images so strong that he was having trouble in processing them.

One day he went out in the kayak to check on a fishnet that he had set at the mouth of the river. It was a sinking gill net, whose lead line rested on the shingle bottom that gradually sloped from the shore. Tik paddled up the length of the net to see if any fish were caught. Silver shapes struggled beneath him, jerking the green plastic floats that held the net upright in the water. Toward the shallow end of the net, the floats were on the surface, and at this end of the net, two large char were caught, their orange bellies floating out of the water. Tik grabbed the net to disentangle the fish, then quickly dropped it in disgust. Empty eye sockets. Gulls had pecked out the eyes, leaving the fish grotesquely ugly. He hated gulls. What a horrible act it was, to peck out the eyes of a creature! "But it is wrong to think this way," he told himself. "The gulls just peck at the most conspicuous part first, and this is a survival thing with gulls, behavior that is innate, and normal, totally lacking in malice." And yet he could not overcome his revulsion and loathing of gulls, illogical though it might be. Funny, but he didn't seem to have anything against ravens, and they too were scavengers. Maybe it had something to do with the color of ravens' eyes, which were deep and dark and unfathomable, while the gulls had eyes of shallow, evil, yellow.

One morning when Ipeelee had gone up the hill to spot seals with his old brass telescope, Tik sat in the big tent, muttering irritably, and pumping the Primus stove. Breakfast had been ready for ages, so why the hell couldn't Philip get up? He was always bragging about how he used to go and milk cows and feed pigs and shoot rabbits before breakfast, wasn't he? Nowadays he got up late every day, yet still demanded a piping-hot, unburnt meal to be waiting for him. Tik hummed as he fiddled with the washer on the top of the Primus stove. Butter, he thought, would be as good as anything to grease a pump washer with. He tried butter in his tea once, like the Tibetans, but it tasted awful.

He heard Philip stirring in his tent, then the sound of the tent flaps being tied back, followed by the crunch of boots on shingle. As Philip entered the cook tent, Tik served up a big bowl of porridge, which filled the tent with steam. Freshly made milk was in a jug on the table, and there was a delicious aroma of coffee. Philip sat down without a word and began to eat. He had been writing until late into the night and now had a headache.

"Do you fancy a couple of rashers of bacon, mate? I could have them ready in a jiffy."

Philip looked across at Tik with a sour expression. "For one thing, I am not your mate, and what is more, I wish you would find something to do in the morning while I am getting up. I've got a lot to think about and I can't bear to listen to that horrible moaning singing of yours, which you always seem to do in the morning."

"Sorry." Fuck you. Serve you right for lying in your bloody bag and listening.

"Go and wash the canoe out. It's messy as usual. It stinks. And don't sing."

"OK. The coffee is in the pot." Give yourself an enema with it. Hope it chokes you. Philip grunted and Tik went out of the tent, angry as hell. Yes sir, no sir, three bags full sir. A raven on a rock croaked at him. You can get screwed too, you black-feathered bastard.

He took everything out of the canoe and turned it over on

its side. He and Ipeelee had washed it out, but the past days of hunting and blood, as well as the carrying of meat and blubber, were bound to leave some trace. What the hell! The trouble with Philip was that he thought he could carry on work up here like the old-time European explorers, like Franklin, who expected silver and napkins on the bloody table. All Philip did was fuss about his bloody science, and then worry about his wife and kid, and his work. Bunch of crap. Should have stayed south. That was it — science was a bunch of crap. Tik reflected on that for a while.

Ipeelee came down the hill, telescope under his arm. He was about to speak to Tik, who was hurling buckets of water into the canoe and scrubbing furiously. The seawater beside the canoe was very faintly tinged pinkish with blood. Tik didn't see him, and then Ipeelee saw that Tik was muttering, in a barely audible low monotone. What was this? A spell for good luck? But the young man's face was full of anger, his brow furrowed. Worried now, the old Inuit walked quietly around him.

Sunday. Philip wanted to write letters. He gave Tik the task, or rather the ultimatum, to wash his clothes. On previous occasions when Tik had been told to do his laundry, he had merely spread his clothes out on the beach, a little way up from low tide, and had weighted them with stones. His theory was that the coming and going of the tide over a few days would get them clean enough. Philip did not agree. However, when Tik actually got down to the job, it didn't take too much time because he wore so little, and changed so infrequently. He finished, and spread the clothes out on rocks to dry, then went to sit beside Ipeelee down by the shore, bringing the old man a mug of tea, very black and very sweet, as he liked it.

"Three days from now, Ooniak will come," said Ipeelee.

"The hunt has been successful. Now they must wait at a headland to make a little repair to the engine."

"How do you know?" asked Tik.

The old man did not answer such a foolish, and somewhat rude, question.

"When he comes, we will hunt beluga. It would be better if Tikkisi could come with us, but it would not be good to ask that one, he would become angry. There will be other hunts." He smiled at Tik, who sat, saddened by the thought of Ipeelee's leaving.

"This man prays for a good hunt for his father Ooniak and his grandfather Ipeelee," said Tik, proud that he could now say such a complicated sentence. The old man nodded. He could feel the beluga out there, yet knew that he must not think of the hunt, for the beluga would sense his dreams and escape. Tik finished his tea and went up to Philip's tent.

"Phil? Can I go out in the kayak? I'd like to check on that peregrine's nest on the cliffs just outside the inlet."

"OK," came the answer from inside the tent, "but don't go offshore, and be back in time to get supper."

Tik headed out through the mouth of the inlet, and saw that now the ice had been scattered. Seafowl, ducks, mergansers, guillemots and the occasional loon, were feeding or flying about the bay. Tik had not eaten much, and his stomach rumbled. He felt in his anorak pocket and found half a bar of chocolate and his harmonica.

Despite the sunshine, there was a chill in the air, and unlike other days, no warm breezes came from the land to carry with them the faint scents of vegetation. Neither was the ice melting, no water dripping with the sounds of a million bells. He paddled past the cliffs, and the falcons swooped down. Indeed, the falcons had young, for he could hear the faint piping up there above him in the rocks. Not wishing to disturb them further, and against Philip's orders, he paddled farther out into the bay.

Instead of the .22, he had brought the shotgun with him today. He had brought it because on days like this, when he felt a little mad inside, he liked the big booming bang and the satisfying kick of the gun. He brought it out, loaded it, checked the safety catch, and laid it on the taut splash cover, under a couple of tied thongs. A couple hundred yards away, a little flock of guillemots swam in the lee of a large floe. Tik headed toward them until he got close enough, then laid the paddle in front of him and took up the gun. He made a mental note to himself not to fire the gun anywhere except over the bow, because once before he had followed the flight of a duck and fired the gun to the side, almost overturning the kayak with the recoil. The little birds had seen the strange shape gliding toward them, and were disturbed. As soon as the shape came into range, a shot boomed, and the flock dove, leaving two floating dead on the surface. Tik turned the kayak with one paddle stroke, waited still, then blasted a surfacing bird thirty yards away. With twin metallic pops, the ejected cartridges flipped out of the gun, and stayed upright in the water, bobbing like red fishing floats. Tik closed the gun and slipped it under the splash cover. It was enough.

The guillemots looked so pathetic, with their little red feet, smaller even than those of an old-squaw duck, lying upwards. Tik grabbed them, and with a quick jerk he pulled their heads off and held the bodies over the side to drain the blood into the water.

Birds were beginning to settle again after the shock of the reverberating gunshots. Now, having done his killing, and with supper assured, Tik wanted only to watch them. In the death of a wild creature there is a sad, lonely poetry that hunters are rarely insensitive to. Tik paddled from the place of killing, farther out from the land.

In the summer sea, ice pieces drifted like great white swans. A loon flew swift toward the shore, and bird cries broke the silence. On the sea, as still as a pond, he paddled lazily, with no haste to land. The kayak shadow glided like a ghost. Forgetting hunger, he moved among the blue white ice swans, wondering at their strange calmness, undisturbed by noisy seafowls that swam in their shadows. Were there, wondered Tik, such things as ice spirits? On a day like this, the sea and the ice that moved upon it in graceful ballet looked so peaceful and benign, yet should the wind suddenly change, the ice would form ranks and lines and phalanxes and move through the water to crush and drown him. While at the same time appreciating and enjoying serenity, Tik felt at that moment that he would like to battle with the ice spirits, to joust with them, to dodge them, and as he made his fantasies he felt an inexplicable sensation of having passed backwards through dimensions of great time, into the consciousness of a former life. He felt as if this day had been the first that he had been out on the sea, among the ice forms. He blinked his eyes at the diamond points of reflecting sunlight that made interlinking crosses through the lenses of his eyes. He looked around to see if there were any seals about, not because he thought of hunting right then, but because he felt he would like to see a funny, whiskered face peering so seriously out of the water and looking at him with those big, mournful brown eyes.

But really, had this Tik creature once before moved among the ice forms in a previous life, perhaps not even a human life? Water, ice, solid, liquid, transparent, white, formless and formed, and all the same. Tik's mind spun around on itself, and for a frightening moment he saw evil things pushing up from inside, and he imagined consciousness leaving him, mindless, wandering out farther from land, never, never to return. Momentarily, he thought that once he had sprung from a form that had feared land, and that this thing, remnant within him, drew him to the Sea Mother. A word of Welsh came unexpectedly to his lips, and he struggled for its meaning but it blew away. A cat's paw of wind. He snapped back, out of this daydream, but still the quiet and the lack of seals bothered him, and he felt the need of sound. Human sound. Remembering the harmonica, he took it from the pocket of his anorak and tapped fluff out of it. How those thin little reeds could wail and echo! Even at this distance from shore, the rocky hills and cliffs caught and held the notes, throwing them back so that notes wove into each other, coming and going, loud and soft. Tik let the paddle rest in front of him and played blues, cupping the harmonica in both hands so that he could wail and muffle.

In Ipeelee's assessment of things, there was no such thing as coincidence. To him, all things were interrelated. When the terrified pod of beluga porpoised through the narrow mouth of the inlet and into its sheltered confines, Ipeelee knew that they came here because something extremely powerful drove them here, whether it were magic, fear, or both. There were twenty of them, and they went from one length of the inlet to the other, filling the underwater places with their trilling voices. Even from inside his tent, Philip heard their above-water sounds — the powerful venting of steamy breath that hung in the cold still air like misty feathers. Knowing that this coming of the beluga was of great significance, Ipeelee ran up past the tents, trying to reach a high point from where he could see. Philip, too, was out of his tent, and he followed the old man.

From the top of the ridge they could look down into the

clear waters of the inlet where the white shapes of the adults and the smaller gray shapes of the young beluga could be seen in crystal definition. Philip began to count them and pull out his notebook, but Ipeelee was pulling at his sleeve, making him look to the other side, out in the open bay.

Even at the top of the ridge, sounds came faintly to them. To the old man it was a wondrous, magical sound. Ipeelee had heard men play harmonica before, but never those dipping, wailing notes, with ghostly echoes repeating the sounds like an incantation. Yet even these wondrous sounds were not the focal point of Ipeelee's attention, for out in the bay, six killer whales blew and circled the kayak, their fins black against the golden glare of sun off water, and the plumes of their breath catching light.

Tik had seen the whales coming from afar, and he had guessed that it was his harmonica music that attracted them. Then, when they drew close, he recognized the big bull by the way his dorsal fin flopped at the tip, and he felt as if he were seeing an old friend. One by one, the whales passed by the kayak, rolling to one side so that they could see him more easily. Then they all swam around him, surfacing in twos and threes and blowing with a strong, almost musical rhythm. They were making sounds too, and Tik realized that he really could hear them, even feel them, resonating through the thin hull of the kayak. He played on and on, trying to match the rhythm of their breathing with his music, and sometimes bowing his head down into the cockpit of the kayak, so that the sound would be amplified and carried into the water from this taut shell of wood and canvas. Water swirled around them. He felt drunk, elated. Light flickered in his eyes and the breaths of the whales were golden flames. His lips were dry, and he lowered the harmonica, staring now at the shapes mov-

ing around him, gazing into the intelligence of eyes that gazed
unblinkingly back at him, watching the delicate, almost sen-
sual, opening and closing of the big animals' blowholes. Light
flickered, changing with the surface swirls, and the watcher
became the watched, the center of a dance, and Tik entered
a state of ecstasy, wanting more than anything to join the
dance and grow with these colors that changed to sounds and
filled him, filled him completely. He did not notice the harmonica slip from his fingers, slither down the canvas and drop
into the water, where it dipped and weaved downwards, en-
thralling a juvenile female who took it several times into her
mouth and dropped it again, and watched the sparkle of the
metal sides lessen as the green of the sea closed out light.

By the time Ipeelee and Philip reached him in the freighter
canoe, Tik was indeed deep in a trance. They had to shake
him, and actually lift him out of the kayak before the trance
was broken, and even after that he sat with staring eyes, saying
nothing.

The whales had gone, leaving as soon as the angry, buzzing
noises of the outboard engine had reached them. Engines
meant bullets, boats, and even though men up here rarely
bothered them, it was within the memory of the leader of the
pod that boats sometimes meant pain originating from the surface things. Bullets rarely killed, but they could fester, cause
great pain, and sometimes even death from blood poisoning.
He had called his family and sped away, forgetting about the
trapped beluga, and searching now for more.

It was obvious to Philip that there was no point in talking
to Tik until they got back to camp, and besides, he was too
angry to risk his rage at the youth right now. Ipeelee too was
silent, but he was silent because words were not called for. He
saw enough in the boy's face. He had been right.

Directly after a supper that he had to cook himself, Philip began to dismantle the kayak. Tik was washing dishes. Ipeelee watched Philip. The old man thought that the white man now understood the danger that the boy faced, understood that the boy was not yet strong enough to control the magic that was channeled through him. To Ipeelee, who understood these things, it was obvious that the boy did not really know what he was doing when he called the whales, nor did the boy see that their calling of him might prove to be stronger. Had the talking that the whales poured into the boy's mind gone on any longer, they might have persuaded him to come with them, down deep into the sea to talk with the many-named one, Luma, the sea goddess, who carried the souls of many a hunter in the hood of her *amautik*. Yes indeed, the big white man was doing the wisest thing for a white man to do — he was depriving Tikkisi of his kayak until his spirit became stronger. Had that one been Inuit, then Ipeelee would have insisted that the two of them bind the boy, tie him, so that he, Ipeelee could make strong protective spells. But a white man would never understand the need for this and no man could bind the boy now. No, the white man did the best thing. However, thought Ipeelee, this old man must talk more seriously and deeply with the boy, and try to teach him chants of power, or disaster of a terrible kind might overtake them all.

To Philip, it was more simple. Tik had disobeyed him and could not be trusted. The kayak would be dismantled and would stay dismantled until the end of summer, and that was that.

Tik came out of the tent and saw what was happening.

"Hey! Quit that." He rushed up and snatched away a strut that Philip was putting into the longer of the two bags that the folding kayak came in. Tik shouted at Philip, saying that it was his kayak, his. With horror, Ipeelee watched as the two men struggled with each other, both yanking on the strut. With a crack, it broke, and Tik fell backwards onto the shingle. Coming to his feet with a scream of rage, he rushed at the bigger man, trying to push him away from his kayak, his most precious possession, now lying collapsed and dismantled, with its hull lying like a fish, flayed, boned, limp.

"You lousy, rotten bastard, get away!"

Like a bear cuffing a cub, Philip swung his open hand at Tik's head. Although not meant to injure, the blow was struck in anger, and it carried enough force to knock Tik to the ground, ears ringing. He got up slowly, shaking his head, mouth twitching, eyes filling with tears. He saw Ipeelee looking at him and felt shame, yet even more, rage.

"Yes, old man, that one is a bear, a big bear, but this one will kill him if he touches this one again."

Horrified, Ipeelee wanted to leave, walk away from this foreign violence, yet he could not, for he felt compassion for the boy, and in truth, he even admired the simple strength of the one they called Nanook. For Nanook did what he had to do, yes, indeed.

After Philip went away, Ipeelee took the two broken pieces of kayak strut and set about figuring the best way to fix it. His seamed, weathered face, deep in concentration as he handled the two pieces of wood, reflected a great and wonderful kindness.

⇜ SEVEN ⇝

And so it was, very early the next day, that Ipeelee shook Tik awake and bade him follow him, to a high point a mile's walk from camp.

"Where do we go?" asked Tik, hurrying after the old man.

"To a place of vision, where a man can see far, where many of the Inuit have sat and watched, and where some still stay and wait."

They reached the top of the hill, which from a distance had not appeared to be that good as a vantage point, but which from the top commanded a 360 degree view of hills, ridges, lakes and sea. The two men sat down and Ipeelee took out his pipe.

"This old and foolish man does not know the words of the white man," began Ipeelee, "but the words of the Inuit carry much power. You, Tikkisi, are clever, and in a short space of time you have learned to speak our language well. Yet you do not understand the strength of our language. This old and foolish man hopes and tries to wish away the words that you let escape from you when you said you would kill Nanook."

"I was angry," said Tik. "It is the nature of white men."

"Hah!" said Ipeelee. "Does Tikkisi think that the Inuit are always smiling, always harmless, like lemmings? Does he think that the Inuit do not know anger? Let this one tell you a story. Many seasons past, before the white men came, this old man, who was young then, saw his brother killed by another and more powerful man, who harpooned the brother and dragged him across the snow on the end of the line to be butchered with a snow knife. Yes, and this one's brother's wife was taken away by the murderer, who killed to take her."

"Why did you not fight for your brother?" asked Tik.

"A boy of seven years does not fight well," answered Ipeelee.

"Seasons passed, and this one grew stronger and taller, and our people went over to the big land to hunt caribou, for the year was bad for seal. We traveled many miles inland, and there we met another people, also Inuit, but Inuit who hunted only caribou and who spoke with strange accents, with words we did not know. This one learned many things among these people, things which you could use."

"In a . . ." Tik fumbled for a word and then found it, "in a book I have read of those people. They hunt the caribou and kill them in rivers with a spear."

"Yes, those Inuit knew many things, some of which my people knew, and some which we did not. But they taught Ipeelee to find the killer of a brother, how to search out his breath. With the power, I killed him, caused him to run naked into the sea, in the dark months. He ran into an open lead, and was gone. His wife wept."

"Did you frighten him? Chase him with a spear?"

The old man laughed. "No, no, I reached out with my mind and ate his soul."

"How?"

"Does Tikkisi fear death?"

"No."

The old man then came and sat on the ground before Tik, sitting so close that their knees touched. Softly, he began to chant, and Tik at first felt embarrassed, and wanted to move, but the old man held him by the shoulders, forcing him to stay. The words were at first without meaning to Tik, but the old man kept on and on, chanting, with the sound coming from both belly and throat, reverberating, resonant, until it split into two voices, and all the while the old man kept staring, and holding Tik until the crow's feet, and the many other lines of the old man's face metamorphosed into arrows, an etched pattern that led to the depths of his eyes. Tik was held, held until the words began to come through him, and despite their simplicity, Tik began to shudder and tremble.

Aiyah! Aiyah!
His secret name
He thought hidden in his breast,
But in my drum-song I shout,
In his brain I blow.
From his soul I suck
Life force.
Aiyah! Aiyah!
This man steals the name.
He weakens, he seeks me in his dreams.
He runs to the hilltop
Catching sight of shadows.
Aiyah! Aiyah!
He cannot see my face
Or speak my name.
My name is hidden in the bird skin
Of my totem.
We now share the same soul place.

Hah! I push him out!
Cold tears at his belly!
Aiyah! Aiyah!
This man does not die,
But already, in that one's eye
Maggots thrive.
Madness takes joy,
Crows bloated with power,
Takes great happiness
In the stench
Of death-flesh.
Aiyah! Aiyah! Aiyah! Aiyah!
His secret name
He thought hidden in his breast . . .

Tik trembled, and experienced a horror, not of the twentieth century, but of a time when squat, brown hunters moved in migrations from the vast Asian continent, a time when all things continued, were linked by a multidimensional web extending into past, future, present, and into the worlds of dreams.

"Does Tikkisi fear death?" asked Ipeelee again.

"Yes," whispered Tik, in English.

"Then Tikkisi must take responsibility for his words, so carelessly spat out. Tikkisi must suck them back out of the air and digest them, lest they run and hide and wait to do evil, like the *tornait* of the windy places. Truly, that one is a bear, and bear is his known name and not his secret name, but still there is power in the words of our language. He is a bear, but also a man who believes in his heart that he does only good things for you, remember that. He has pain, too, to see a young boy grow away and change, remember that."

Tik, still trembling, nodded.

"Does Ipeelee not fear death?" He felt compelled to ask. The old man shook his head and pointed to a far-off hill, shaped like a dome.

"Over there is an ancient resting place of our people, where many lie." He began to recite the names of long-dead Inuit to Tik, holding him by the shoulders as he did so.

"My father died many years before the white man came to these islands, as did my brother. But my father died smiling, and singing, for to him his death was of little meaning. He had power, and dying to him was not dying, but changing. Now, this day, his eyes can be seen in the eyes of many of our people. His laughter can be heard. The things he taught come to us when we do not expect them to come. Yet he is buried over there, on that hill, beside the woman they called Kila Umiapik, a woman also of power, whose eyes shine in the face of Annie, this one's granddaughter. The Inuit should not put their dead beneath the soil with the ever-present frost and with the worms of darkness! No! The worms of the air change to grow wings! The Inuit must put their dead where the wind can blow, so that their souls might see which way to travel. No, this old man Ipeelee does not fear death, for he has many songs of power."

And then Ipeelee began to chant again, and although held in mute terror of the old man, Tik also felt a compelling peace. The words washed over him.

> *Aiyah! Aiyah!*
> *This man's name will be remembered.*
> *Aiyah! Aiyah!*
> *This man's name will be remembered.*
> *Aiyah! Aiyah!*
> *This man's spirit*
> *Will not be contained by stones.*

Aiyah! Aiyah!
With the wind it will be blown
Among the grave mounds
And by the marker cairns
And across the bay
To the place where the gray
Of water-sky
Dips to the offshore lead.
Aiyah! Aiyah!
This man's spirit
Will see the ringed seal,
Taste his liver and heart,
The sweetness of his warmth
And the joy of past hunting times.
Aiyah! Aiyah!
And on the point, from the camp,
Comes the cry
Of a baby.
Aiyah! Aiyah!
This man's spirit will fly
Toward the crying
And enter through the mouth.
Aiyah! Aiyah! Aiyah!
This man's name will be remembered.
Aiyah! Aiyah!

He had been sleeping. His legs were numb. The old man gently slapped his face. "Come Tikkisi, we will go to our tent and make tea." He helped Tik stand. "This old man has only two more days in the camp. Come here, very early, each morning. Understand? Then, when Ipeelee has gone, still come here, for this old man can speak to some men across great distance."

Tik nodded, and the two walked down over ridges smoothed by ancient ice, with rounded contours covered in patches by carpets of moss, lichens, and hardy grasses; around hollows that were boggy or pond filled, where old-squaw ducks and mergansers swam with their young, and where phalaropes dallied, making patterns on the water. The days raced away. The old man was worried, for he needed a lot more time, time to let the balm of the words wrap around the boy's wounds, give him a cocoon in which to grow and strengthen. Aieee! These white men were so brittle!

The Inuit Peterhead returned, and Ipeelee was gone, happy with the money he had earned, and with the small fortune in seal skins that were being prepared at Neviaksi's camp. But he was troubled by the aura of hostility that he was leaving behind. Danger lurked in such hostility, and men who felt that way should not be in camp alone together — they should be separated, or have children and women and dogs and laughter around them. In the camps of the Inuit, one of them would be forced to travel, or in the old days, their disagreements would have been fought out in song, with the protagonists battling with taunts and words and clever innuendoes, beating hand drums and making the rest of the camp reel with laughter. This one, this boy Tikkisi, he was like all men of laughter, carrying another face of grief and anger, a face which he was releasing more and more frequently. Aieee! We would not have called him Boy-who-smiles had we met him now, thought Ipeelee.

Because he was worried, Ipeelee had got Ooniak to ask permission of Philip to allow Tik to hunt beluga with them for a week, but this had been flatly, almost angrily, refused, and the Inuit retreated into masks of affable inscrutability. They no longer liked Philip. Unfortunately, Tik knew of the request and suffered his disappointment in enraged silence. It was strange that he never considered leaving without permission, for he still felt a binding sense of duty to the big man. It was a pity too that he seemed incapable of arguing with Philip. Philip could turn words around, and Tik would find himself saying things he did not mean in order to defend previous thoughts and statements. Also, when he tried to argue, the muscles of his face would tighten, and the corners of his mouth would turn down and twitch, and he would find himself incapable of speaking at all. One trouble was, perhaps, that he would begin by trying to defend a principle or an idea, and find within minutes that he was defending himself. Tik did not feel confident to joust with Philip on a mental plane, and so he retreated more and more into silence, which was interpreted by Philip as sulkiness.

Then, in turn, Philip began to mold small inconsiderations and lack of civility into small cruelties, all accepted without comment, and all remembered.

One early morning in late July, Philip went out to hunt a seal which had wandered into the inlet. He took the freighter canoe and shotgun. With one hand he steered the canoe, and with the other he held the shotgun up to his shoulder, blasting away. Each time the seal surfaced, the water was patterned with shot around its head. Range and angle were bad, for Philip fired seven times, and yet still the seal lived and dived.

Tik sat in the door of the tent. Rocks, wet with dew. Sun barely risen over the low hills. Stove hissing, and the porridge plopping with bubbles of steam. Tik was irritated at the sight of this hunt, for if they had done it together, with one man at the tiller and the other in the bow with a gun, the seal would have been taken by now. He was irritated too by the echoing crash of the gun, by the whining buzz of the motor, and by the laughing cries of disturbed gulls. He picked up the .270, which was just inside the tent, and rammed a shell into the breach, slipping off the safety catch with his thumb. Kneeling, he aimed at the distant spot which was the seal's head. It was really too far. Could he hit it? He would have to hit it for sure. The rifle had fine sights, and its bullet left the barrel when fired with power, speed, flat trajectory. He was almost sure, but he hesitated, just in time for Philip's last barrel of SSG shot to pierce the seal's brain with one lethal shot. Damn! Without thinking, and like a kid playing a war game, Tik shifted the aim of the gun, looking at Philip through the peep sights as he gaffed in the seal. Sweat suddenly broke out on his face and chest, and he realized that his finger was tightening on the trigger. He pushed the gun away from him and sat down, looking at the ground, shaking and crying. The sounds of the outboard faded into the distance, and Tik saw that Philip had headed out of the inlet. He rarely told Tik what he was going to do nowadays.

"Damn him anyway," said Tik to himself. "I should have shot the bastard!"

He went into the tent and turned the stove off, and as the hiss of escaping gas died, Tik heard silence.

Then, with shocking loudness, a loon screamed over the water. Tik sucked in breath, picked up the rifle again and went out of the tent once more. It sat a hundred and fifty yards out on the water, a black, white-dashed shape on a surface as smooth as polished metal. That cry again! It wailed from out of the depths of his past. The loon dived and emerged again, rising like a spirit out of the water, neck stretched and beak pointed to the sky. Tik steadied the rifle on a rock and framed the bird clearly in the ring of the sight. He squeezed off the shot and saw water explode behind the bird. He ejected the spent cartridge and put the rifle away. Something black and still floated out there, and now Tik remembered that he could not retrieve it, for he had no kayak. The body floated toward the mouth of the inlet.

From down the inlet, another loon came, flying like an arrow, loon-swift, settling on the water with a long splash. It looked at the dead thing. Bright red streamers waved and undulated from the decapitated neck, and near the body a few small gray feathers, tipped with black, floated like tiny gondolas. A slight breeze hurried over the inlet, scattering the little fleet of curved gray feathers. The living bird dived and swam underwater for a long distance. When it came up it wailed that banshee cry . . . "tooooooodleeeeeeee!" And Tik sat down on the beach, his muscular shoulders shaking with awful sobs.

The nights became oppressive, and he could not sleep, not that night, not for several nights following the murder of the loon. He felt that should he die now, there would be neither loss nor meaning in his death. He existed on the fringe of things, living like a parasite on the country he longed to be a part of. He was like a ghost, out of sequence, an unreal being vibrating at a different frequency from the things around him, which were hidden by veils he could not pierce. Indeed, he wished that this body of his would dematerialize, so that he could move invisible among the wild and free things! His morning meditations at the top of Ipeelee's hill gave him small peace, and the old man's eyes grew distant, and Philip was always down there, always needing his hot breakfast and clean canoe and filled lamp and oiled rifle and, and, and, and, and . . .

Then, when Tik walked over the tundra, he heard strange things. He heard buses and church bells and voices. He thought of suicide, but did not like the feel of the rifle barrel in his mouth, the cold hardness of it, and the foresight hurting his gums. He did not like the image of his brains blown though the back of his head, a red and gray porridge like the brains of the seal that Philip had clubbed with his great fist. No, not that! But still, he knelt there with the rifle, by the Inuit cairn, looking out over the sea, thinking of the difference between living and dying, and seeing no great merit in either.

A raven followed him. Ravens seemed to have been following him all his life, selecting him specifically for observation and comment. Raven . . . sometimes he gives a pure, bell-like note, and this, thought Tik, is an echo of his wanting to be believed. Bird of cunning. Bird of legend. Bird of fate. Bird of death. The myths say that once the raven was white as snow, and that he became black because he lied. But this is foolishness, the raven never lied, he pecked out the eyes from the spiked heads of kings and criminals with equal impunity, for he never lied. Tik knew that the raven had not lied to him as the loon had lied. It was not the raven who had cried out sounds of unattainable freedom, sounds of impossible soul flight. No, it was not the raven. No lying. No flying. Would lying then imply a knowledge of truth? Could it be? If so, then perhaps the loon had not lied either, and it was himself, Tik, Tikkisi, Richard Tavett, who saw deception in that shout.

"I have a liar's ears, liar's eyes, liar's nose, and this is truly a terrible thing, for through these organs the whole world becomes a lie!" And he wondered over and over if he should be dead, and wondered if life should not be one, clear note, a bell tone.

". . . raven, haven, dead, said, eye, lie, me, see, wait, hate, myth . . ." They marched in pairs through his mind, stamping, reverberating, beating colored footprints, strange scents to his nostril, trains of forgotten Welsh phrases, tumbling sequences of the language of the Inuit, snatches of Ipeelee's terrible, double-voiced chanting. . . .

Three days after he had murdered the loon, he heard a bell, yes, a bell, out there on the tundra. But when he looked up it was not a bell, but a raven, a raven bell, hanging up there in the sky on his old black feathers. Raven was a watcher for the sky god, just as the gulls were the spies of evil things. They deceived. Color roles reversed.

Tik ran, stumbling through water-logged mosses at the edge of a pond, thinking about it all, and about the oppressive thing in his chest which lay like a great stone. Poor old raven. It was not raven but the angels who were a lie, for if they could really fly they would have pectoral muscles sticking out four feet in front of them. Run. He was wearing rubber boots, and he got water in them, and they started to make disgusting sucking noises. His mind was spiraling off in associations, and he began to sing a song to himself, making up words to pull his mind back. Why couldn't the raven realize that he had a one-note bell soul? Why all that discord, that croaking? But the ravens didn't care, they went on stunting and playing in the upcurrents of the cliff, ignoring the strangely behaving boy.

But this was real-time, not dream-time, and Tik ran on, chest heaving, vision blurring with the effort. He cried out for help, wondering what it was that chased him, or what he chased after, for whatever it was, it truly existed, somewhere, on some plane. Philip, the camp, and everything about it became distant, and Tik looked up at the sky as if to see the spirit form of the loon, but he had come down from a high place and the sky was stolen by cliffs which rimmed the narrowing gulley he had entered. Now, a glaucous gull followed him, circling overhead and laughing, leering down with those nasty yellow eyes, eyes in the sky, surrounded by feathers of white purity. Tik fired a shot that whapped through the wing feathers but did not bring the gull out of the sky. He, Tik, would declare war on all gulls. Another two shots clipped through the gull's feathers before it veered off. At last Tik stopped running and collapsed by a stream to drink. He was miles from camp. He lay on his belly and watched a shoal of sticklebacks moving over the sandy stream bed like a hundred pieces of spiny, enameled jewelry. After a while he rolled over and watched clouds in the sky, letting the earth move under him, thinking of a long-ago girl, thinking sex thoughts.

Soon after the day of his Declaration of War upon Gulls, Tik escaped camp to go hunting for the pot. He killed a duck on a pond, and with the sound of the shot, a gull came up from the south, a large glaucous gull that settled on the water and began tugging at the dead duck. Tik scared it off with his angry and erratic shot, but it didn't go far. Wind blew the duck to the pond and Tik retrieved it, putting it into his game bag before he continued his walk. The gull followed, flying overhead and scolding with a persistent four-syllable chuckle, warning game of Tik's approach. Hunting became fruitless, and Tik became infuriated. He shook his fist.

"You miserable, nagging, scavenging hag! I see you there, aloof in the sourness of your flesh, you aggravating, hateful bitch, hanging over my head like a bad deed, taunting me, mocking me. You filthy old bitch, go away!"

The gull chuckled, "Kyeah, kyeah, kyeah, kyeah!"

If you cut open a gull's gizzard you find it full of old fish bones and muck. The last one Tik had opened contained the toenails and broken bones of a young guillemot. The entrails had smelled bad, sour and sickening, even though the gull was freshly killed. Gulls glide up in the sky and people proclaim their beauty, but if you look at their guts you discover the sourness. Look into their eyes, and see unthinking cruelty.

The gull followed Tik for an hour, cackling his presence to the tundra. Tik walked close to the beach, watching the gull's flight. It would dip against the wind until it stalled, then hang motionless for a split second. Tik timed the dips and stalls, seeing that they were regular, and then he fired on the next stall, hearing his bullet smack through the wing bone, close to the body. The gull spun out of the air like a sycamore seed, its fall followed by a few white feathers scattering in the wind. When it hit the water, Tik was sure that he had it, but instead of lying there helplessly, it began to swim away, out of range, bouncing on the waves. He fired shot after shot and emptied the magazine of the .22, but the bullet kept hitting in front of or behind the target. But what the hell? It was only a dirty gull, and crippled like that it would not live long. He left the beach and went on hunting.

The sky was blackish gray and the light poor, and great banks of cumulus rolled in from the northwest. Tik jumped from boulder to boulder along a jumbled beach and scrambled up to the top of a cliff that overlooked a long pond. Behind, in the gray light, the camp seemed to sulk, and the tents were tiny little beasts, huddled down among the rocks. Tik crouched, scanning the water with his binoculars. There were no ducks on the pond, but around the edge a purple sandpiper busied itself, dipping its beak with short, sharp movements like those of a fussy old woman tidying up scraps from the best carpet. Philip had sent him to observe the movements of a certain pair of old-squaw ducks that had a nest somewhere near this place. It was only a few hundred yards from the camp. The pond was ruffled by eddies of wind in the hollow, and small waves lapped against the sphagnum moss around the far edge. A low, deep rumble was carried on the slightly changing wind, sheets of lightning lit distant clouds, and raindrops began to speckle the pond. Tik turned to run back to camp. Rain followed and enveloped him.

"Old Joe God is in a bad mood tonight," he muttered, glancing upward, missing his footing, slipping, and barking his shins.

He reached the comparative dryness of the tent and ducked under the overlapping end of the fly sheet. Lightning tore the sky, great forks of it coming down like the limbs of dead trees, thunder rolling. Tik put on an oilskin and ran up to Philip's tent, which now glowed faintly, the pressure lamp hissing.

"Want anything?"

"No, just check the guy ropes. It will probably get rougher."

Tik did this chore quickly, then ran back to the big tent and ducked in through the door. He took off the oilskin, bundled it up and threw it on the floor. Nowadays his untidiness was practiced. Great wet patches stained the roof, because the old fly sheet leaked. He brewed himself some tea and listened to the rain pounding a tattoo on the canvas, enjoying the soft yellow light of the hurricane lamp that closed in the little world around him, giving the tent an impression of warmth. Canvas walls look less frail when the outside light does not shine through them. The fly sheet strained its ropes, writhing over the tent and the ridgepole like a tortured manta.

Tik had started thinking of walking out of camp, leaving Philip, heading north to join Clyde. But he couldn't contemplate such an action in this weather. He would wait, he thought to himself, for a few more days.

The rain stopped during the night, but the wind began to strengthen. After breakfast Philip put on his yellow rain pants, his thick duffel parka, and the life jacket that could be inflated with a carbon dioxide cartridge. Tik was washing dishes.

"Drop what you're doing and get the canoe ready for me. The gas tank is only a third full, and the canoe has to be bailed out. There's six inches of rainwater in it."

"Surely you're not going out!" Tik protested. "It will be as choppy as hell out there today, and you won't see any seals!"

"Just do what you're told! I want to go out to the islands."

"I'll come with you."

"I don't need you."

Tik dried his hands on a dish cloth. "It's safer with two."

Philip stood in the door of the tent, hunched over because of his height. In the bulky clothing he was huge. Tik gazed into Philip's eyes and saw, for the first time, that Philip was going out in the canoe in the wind and rough water just to prove he could do it, and he didn't want Tik along in case Tik should see the struggle going on within him.

"Phil, I think you're being quite stupid. You are forever climbing up on your pedestal and accusing me of doing stupid and irresponsible things, but look at yourself for a change. If you really have to go out to the islands today, and if it really is too vital and important and urgent to let it wait until the wind dies, then I insist that I come too."

He tried to squeeze past Philip, intending to get his own rain gear, but as he did so, Philip pushed him, hard, sending him sprawling.

"That doesn't scare me!" said Tik. "I can see you now. Under all that size, you're just a big bullying coward!" He got up and again tried to push past, but this time Philip seized his clothing, bunching up the cloth in his fist. Tik had never seen him so angry, and he shook Tik.

"You sniveling little pipsqueak! Get out there and do as

132

you're told! I could have chosen a hundred lads who would have been far more use to me than you, but I thought you had the makings of a scientist, so I gave you a chance! Now, go and get that tank filled, and bail out that boat. Just keep your puny little thoughts to yourself!"

Now Tik was enraged. "Go shove the tank and the canoe up your scientific arsehole! And let go of me or I'll . . ."

With ease, Philip lifted Tik until he was on his toes, bringing his face close, so that Tik could see the tiny veins in his eyes, the blue of the lids, wrinkles, a mole on the chin, near the mouth, under the hairs of the beard. Tik was really scared now, but the icy ball of fury grew in his belly. Philip was sneering at him.

"Or you'll what?"

Ipeelee's warning flashed into his mind, but still the words came out in a tremulous, tight-lipped whisper.

"You will die."

With a snort of contempt, Philip hurled the youth from him, out the door of the tent. "Go away, little boy, I can do things for myself!"

Tik picked himself up and went to the store tent. He could hear Philip clomping about outside, lifting things into the canoe, banging boxes and equipment against the sides. Wind buffeted the walls of the tents, gusts going up to twenty and twenty-five miles an hour and seeming to increase. Tik sat on a red box. He was so angry he wanted to scream with rage. He shut his eyes tight and watched scarlet spirals spinning in deep purple. There was a bitter taste in his mouth. Ammunition box. He unscrewed the lid and looked at its contents, his eyes not focusing properly. Shotgun shells, red and blue cartridges with brass caps — dust shot for collecting small birds, shot numbers six, five, four, two, SSG, buckshot. Rifled slugs, heavy enough to stop a bear. Rifle ammunition, dozens of cartons of .22 bullets, both solid and hollow nosed, and boxes of the expensive and deadly .270, long, slim, shiny-new. Tik rummaged through the box and opened cartons of shot shells, and sat there, just staring at them, staring at the backs of cartridges that lay there in their cartons and looked back up at him until the colors of the shells and cartons merged, making patterns like oil on water — red, blue, lead gray and brass yellow. Danger, do not expose to an open flame. Keep out of reach of children. Store in a cool, dry place. Dangerous within one mile. . . . To one side, the shot-gun lay across a box, sniffing at him with its twin nostrils. And suddenly, Tik was seeing things from a great distance, look-ing down on himself as he sat there in the tent in front of the box. And from this distant vantage point, the tent became transparent, he could see into it and out of it, and he floated way up and looked down on the camp and the inlet and the birds and islands in the bay, and the waves and whitecaps, and all the while he was up there, his body was still sitting in front of the box of ammunition, feeling no rage at all.

Very carefully, he selected two twelve-gauge cartridges, one of buckshot and one rifled slug. He loaded the shotgun and went out. Philip was in his own tent now, rummaging around and getting his camera and notebook. With the gun cradled in his arms, Tik stood by the tent. He would come out soon. Tik shifted the position of the gun, caressed the front trigger with his finger, and slid the safety catch forward with his thumb. Time compressed, the whole summer, the summer be-fore, his life in Wales and then in England, and it all went dancing and looping through his brain, a thousand things happening simultaneously. He heard voices calling, church bells ringing, faraway music, brass bands, waves on the shore, canvas flapping, sibilant whispers of wind over rocks and low tundra plants, bird cries. Tik was out-of-body, escaped now from the shackled idiot, and if he could stand straight, truly straight, then surely he would have walked over the water like a Christ. Loons, flying and cackling, laughing like idiots. Why did they laugh? If God made man in his own image, then God is an idiot, with a body that is land-heavy, unable to fly as the loon does, or to cry as the loon does. But no!

Philip came feet first out of the tent, his rump huge in the yellow pants, almost comical. When he turned and saw Tik standing there, with a gun, a look came over his face that was pure amazement.

⌐ EIGHT ⌐

Tik desperately wanted to kill Philip, yet paradoxically, he did not want Philip to be dead. As for Philip, the surprise faded from his face, and he looked at the boy with a sneer.

"You haven't got the guts to do it!"

It was true.

Philip stepped forward, and Tik raised the twin muzzles so that they squinted directly at the older man's face. "Come any closer and I'll blast you!" Time stopped. The man and the boy stood looking at each other, and Tik saw that Philip was not afraid of him, and this made the rage squirm and turn in his guts. To Philip, the drama and anguish of this confrontation was utterly trivial, and the boy could see that in his eyes. Suddenly, the older man leapt at him, knocking the gun to one side and attempting to wrench it from him. But even though Tik was not as big nor as strong as Philip, he was fast and agile. He moved to one side and slammed the butt of the gun against the side of Philip's head. The big man stumbled, went down beside his tent, shaking his head to clear the green lights in his eyes.

136

"Philip! You bastard! I hate you and wish you were dead!" Then Tik raised the gun. He couldn't miss. He jerked both triggers and blasted holes through Philip's tent, missing him by at least two feet. Slowly, Philip stood. He was really big. He walked over to the boy and clubbed him to his knees with a powerful swing of his fist. Bleeding from the mouth and nose, the boy stood up. Philip punched him again, and he fell, the whole earth spinning under him.

Philip looked at the boy, at the holes in his tent, and shook his head. He wanted to pick the boy up, but the anger in him prevented it. He retrieved his camera and went down to the canoe, pausing before he got in to turn his back to the wind and light his pipe.

By the time Tik staggered to his feet, Philip had pushed off in the canoe and was heading into the waves and out into the bay, revving the motor to a furious whine and going much too fast for the sea, so that the canoe bucked and tossed, sending clouds of spray back from the bows to drench him at the stern. The outboard was cavitating, whining and bubbling. Soon the canoe went out of sight, past the headland and out into the bay. Crying in frustration and dull pain, Tik fetched binoculars and went up to the top of the hill, from where he could look out on the storm-torn sea and see his boss, his friend, his teacher, his guru, his hated enemy — way out there, bouncing about on the waves.

Rain squalls beat against the old Inuit marker cairn and plastered Tik's anorak to his skin, stinging his eyes and the swelling on his face. He crouched beside the rock cairn, trying to follow the rain-blurred shape of the canoe, which was now about two miles offshore. Philip was going far too fast, not taking enough notice of counter currents and waves. He had little feel for a boat, nor for the dance and pull of the sea.

Through the binoculars, he watched Philip land on the

137

little islands, which seemed now like white paws clawing at the tattered gray and white blanket of the sea. He saw him have trouble getting off. Damn the stupid fool, he thought, he'll swamp the canoe; and then he began to giggle, to laugh, and he thought that it would teach Philip right, teach him not to insult and ignore and belittle.

"Philip!" he shouted into the winds, "I hope you drown! You hear me? Drown!" He started prancing and hopping about on the top of the hill, round and round the cairn, waving arms and legs and yelling out nonsense songs that were full of childish malice, and even as he sang and yelled and danced, he saw the canoe go side on to the waves. Then the canoe became enveloped in flame, and blossomed like an orange flower upon the waters. The muffled boom of the exploding gas tank took so long to reach Tik that he thought the sound had been eaten by the wind. The canoe burned for a long time, and then it disappeared, and even had he wished to help, there was nothing Tik could do but walk numbly back down to the camp.

Tik was alone now. Completely alone. What could he tell them all when they came to pick them up at the end of the season? How could he face Clyde, or Ipeelee, or Ooniak, or Philip's wife, or Annie? In shock from what he had seen, and from the beating he had received from Philip, Tik could do nothing but take refuge in the performance of established camp routines, and it was around this time of day that he and Philip usually drank tea. Accordingly, he pumped up the Primus, lit a little alcohol in the well, pricked the hole, and fiddled with it until its reassuring blue flame and its comfortable roar began to fill the tent with heat. Tea. Yes, he would make tea for them both. The flame of the kerosene stove flickered and yellowed as the tent walls billowed in and out with the wind. Waves crashed on the beach, and seemed to be trying to pull themselves up to the camp so that they could rampage through it. Spray from the waves spattered the side of the tent which faced the inlet. While the kettle on the stove heated, Tik thought that he should go out and attend to the guy ropes of the tents, so he went out into the rain again. Lightning walked on pointed fingers across the ridges, and in the thunder and howl it seemed to Tik that all this fury was directed against him. He wanted to pray, but couldn't. The shotgun was lying on the ground in the rain. It would get rusty. He picked it up and put it in the store tent. To-morrow, he thought, I'd better remember to clean and oil it. The shot holes in Philip's tent bothered him, and he worried about Philip's stuff getting soaked, but no, that didn't matter anymore, did it?

Numbly, he went about his chores, with tears mingling with rain and salt spray, and running in rivulets down his cheeks. The kettle was taking a long time to boil. Maybe he'd put too much water in it again. Philip was always scolding him about that. He went into the tent and adjusted the valve on the stove. The wet patches on the roof dripped here and there, because the bloody fly sheet leaked like a sieve. He sat down on a box and waited for the kettle to boil.

A gust of wind more powerful than the rest bellied in one wall of the tent and sent the Primus stove rolling, spilling kerosene. Tik snatched at it and burnt his hand. The stove and the top of the table burst into flames, blackening tent canvas, and suddenly Tik felt himself out there in the canoe with Philip, seeing him spill gasoline as he tried to fill the tank, with the wind making the ashes of his pipe blow redly and set fire to the gasoline, flames washing around in the bottom of the canoe, enveloping the gas tank. Tik reacted with speed, ignored the pain of the flames, released the pressure valve on the stove and smothered the flames with an oil-skin jacket.

Now the tent wall was bulging in like a huge paunch, and the ridgepole was cracking and straining and threatening to snap. Tik had to get some of that canvas off. He pushed his way out of the tent and ran around to Philip's tent, shouting for help, shouting for Philip to come, even though he knew it was foolish and childish, for he knew that Philip would not come.

The fly sheet flapped like a living thing, with a loose guy rope lashing like a tail. The wind caught the big square of canvas like a sail on a clipper and pushed upon it with a force that must soon snap the ridgepole. He had to get that damned fly sheet off. It was too big. He had told Philip ages ago that it was too big.

The guy ropes were anchored to rocks on the windward side of the tent, and now they were wire-tight with the strain. Tik reasoned that if he could loosen three more ropes, he could cut the last one and wrestle the fly sheet out of the way. Then the tent would probably stand. The ropes tore at his hands. He got them free, but by the time he reached the last but one rope, his hands were so torn and hurt that he couldn't bear to hold it. He hooked it around his wrist, dug his heels into the shingle and heaved. It came free, but just at that moment the wind got underneath the big square of canvas, ballooning it, snapping the one remaining anchor rope, except that which was still wound tightly around Tik's wrist, and which hurled him over the tent like a doll on a string, bringing him down among the rocks on the leeward side. But of this, Tik knew nothing, nor would he ever know anything.

Ipeelee cut a piece of white *muktuk* from the pile of pieces kept in the tin bath that stood just inside the door of Neviaksi's big tent. There was nothing he liked better than to chew on the delicious, nutty firmness of whale skin, which gave his worn but still strong old teeth something to work on. The hunt had been fortunate indeed, and Neviaksi's camp had plenty of walrus and beluga meat cached for the winter, as well as seal, and the Peterhead, which he, Ooniak and Tommy had come in, was also well loaded with meat, *muktuk,* ivory, and skins for them to carry back to their winter campsite on the mainland. Rain and wind beat against the sturdy tent, and Ipeelee began to hope once more for the gentle strength of snow. Despite the inclement weather outside, however, the tent was warm from the fire of driftwood and blubber that blazed in the stove. Ipeelee glanced over at Annie, troubled to see her so morose, and trembling now. He cut a piece of *muktuk,* a choice piece from near the tail, and carried it over to her, offering it and the little sharp knife that he always carried.

"Eat, little daughter, the storm will soon pass. It is not like you to be afraid of noise in the sky."

"The noise in the sky does not cause me fear, grandfather," she said, listlessly accepting the treat and the knife.

Then, with a jolt, Ipeelee remembered that the excitement of the whale hunt had caused him to forget all about the young white man called Tikkisi, and he too began to listen to the raging storm with new ears.

⇌ NINE ⇌

When he woke, his head hurt. The fur trim of his anorak was stiff with dried vomit. Harsh light clawed at his eyes, and unsteadily, he pulled himself up, hands over his face. He couldn't see straight, and his body felt heavy. His hands were hooked like claws and the skins of the palms rubbed red and raw. Under the hood of the anorak, dried blood stuck the woolen tuque to his head. As soon as he moved, gulls flew from nearby rocks where they had been perching, observing him. Ragged patches of blue sky moved areas of light across the ground, and the wind was beginning to die. He stumbled to his own tent and crawled inside, pain gouging at his head. He thought he would die.

How long had he been lying in the tent? It was past midday, and canvas fluttered with a pleasing rhythm like a train running swiftly over padded rails. As his eyes regained focus, he watched the green cloth of the tent move in and out with the breezes, and he dreamt that he was lying in the belly of a big, breathing animal. Sometimes he could touch the sides with his nose, and sometimes it billowed right out, doubling the inside volume of the tent. A black stain, made by smoke from a badly trimmed hurricane lamp, moved backward and forward, retreating and advancing, a gentle, soothing movement. His skull throbbed, but he was safe inside the breathing, fluttering, green-warm belly. He reached out and drank gratefully from a canteen of water that was always beside his sleeping bag. Pain receded, and he drifted into simple sleep. It had been three days.

The camp was a shambles, with the big tent ripped away from its ridgepole and the heavy fly sheet way over on jumbled rocks on the lee side of the tent. The store tent still stood, but was badly ripped. Only the two pup tents were still standing — the one he slept in, and the other, more expensive one that had been made in Scotland, but that one had shot holes through it, and the holes had been worried and enlarged by the wind. The canoe was gone. Two ravens picked among the ruins of the cook tent, pecking out the remnants of stew from an overturned pot.

Tikkisi drifted in and out of sleep for another two days, waking only to urinate and to take enough water to sustain himself. At the end of it, he half staggered, half crawled, to the nearby stream. His long fast had made him weak, but it had at the same time heightened his senses. Oh, how sweet was the taste of running water! Gently, he pulled back the hood and washed his face, blackened on one side by a huge bruise. To get the woolen hat off he had to go to the first-aid kit in the store tent and find scissors to cut away the blood-matted hair. The wound, a two-inch triangle of contused and torn scalp, was right on the top of his head. He washed it, wincing with pain, and dabbed antiseptic around it. Beside him, the stream gurgled, making happy sounds. The air would cure his wounds.

Ravenously hungry, he searched the supplies for readily eaten food, and found canned meat and hard, crunchy pilot biscuits. The stove still contained fuel, and he heated a billy to make strong, black, sweet tea. Slowly he ate, savoring the wonderful tastes of the food, and as he did so he gave thanks to Toodlik, the sky god, for saving and preserving him. He tried to recount the battle to himself, but his words were badly stuttered, and there were huge blanks, edged with dreams. It could not all have been a dream though, for his hands, with their torn skin, told how valiantly he had struggled, and there was the head wound too. He shuddered to think of the gulls, the witches of the air, waiting around him to make sure he was dead before they pecked out his eyes and sent him sightless on his quest for another body. But he had defeated them so far, and this body was still whole, still his.

Alone now, Tikkisi was prepared to accept the judgment of those benevolent spirits of land, sky and sea. However, he was not prepared to accept the judgment of men, and he knew that to strengthen himself he needed solitude, and he needed to escape quickly from this place of evil.

He assembled the kayak, and in it he scouted away from the inlet, binding his hands with bandages so that he could paddle. There had to be a hiding place, not too distant, yet hard to detect, or perhaps protected in some way. He felt that somewhere in his inner mind, he knew of such a place, and with a map he checked out the indentations of the coast. In three days he found it. It was ideal. His home would be on a long, deep bay that faced to the north, the opposite direction from the bay on which he and the other one had lived. After six hours of kayak travel and four hours of portage, he reached the site. The area promised good hunting, for it had been undisturbed for a long time, and besides, it was far enough away to puzzle searchers. There was a cliff there, under which a deep overhang and a cleft formed a cave, four feet high at the back, seven feet high at the front, and twelve feet deep from the entrance, which was well hidden by a mass of jumbled, frost-cracked boulders which had fallen, over the centuries, from the cliff above. It faced south by southeast and was sheltered enough to encourage low willows and shrubs, giving excellent camouflage. Good. Here he would be safe, and alone.

Now he began to plan the task of bringing enough food and equipment from the old camp to allow him a chance of survival. Each day brought a lessening of the pain in his head, and the coordination in his left arm rapidly recovered from its previous strange weakness that had made it hard to paddle straight.

Back at the old camp, he separated the stuff he would take. He needed a minimum of cooking and eating utensils, but he would use the pressure cooker, one stove, one hurricane lamp, billy cans with dish lids, a cup. He would also take fishing nets and lines, a harpoon and spare head, a float, all manner of rope, an ax, a hatchet, various other tools, knives, a .22 rifle, the shotgun, ammunition, clothing, his own sleeping bag and the bag from the shot-blasted tent, binoculars, and sundry other things like nails and pieces of wire, repair stuff for the kayak. He also took his own sleeping tent and one tarpaulin, leaving three tents behind. He took food and matches, and put aside kerosene in five-gallon jerry cans. Transporting the fuel was a problem, and he really wanted to take both ten-gallon drums, but he could not carry them across the bay in the kayak. They would have to stay, and maybe he could get them later. As it was, he knew he didn't have enough fuel for the winter, but he didn't care.

When he had finished sorting out what he needed, there was a mass of equipment left — three tents, boxes of scientific paraphernalia, preservatives, jars, vials. There was a whole chest of stationery, kit bags of spare clothing (mostly belonging to the other one), pots, pans, an extra stove, a pressure lamp, engine parts, two forty-five-gallon drums of gasoline, a box of paperback books — so much! Why, to take what he needed would mean four separate and careful journeys to the new site. This was a place of madness, greed, and waste. Small wonder that it had been ravaged.

Tikkisi slept one final night at the camp on the inlet. He knew he had to hurry to get out of there, to move his stuff before he was detected. No doubt he would have to return here at times, but he would never linger long. He carried all his stuff and hid it away from the camp, so that he could approach unseen if needed, and take what was his by right of conquest without being interfered with.

The cries of gulls awakened him, making him apprehensive, for they were his enemies and meant him harm. He came out of his tent with caution, the shotgun ready.

Across the inlet, on a point exposed by the falling tide, twenty or more of the yellow-eyed sky witches gathered in rowdy congregation around an object that appeared half in and half out of the water. Through the binoculars, Tikkisi could discern that the object was long, and colored blue and yellow. With an extra box of shotgun shells, Tikkisi launched the kayak and headed across. The water was so calm, and the air so still, that the cries of the gulls came to him in a raucous babble. When he got sixty yards from the point, some of them winged in close to the kayak, but he waited, with cunning, and landed a good distance from the stranded thing. Within him, fear and anxiety battled against his need to know, and as he cautiously approached, his breath came quickly, hands sweated, and the pain in his skull grew. The gulls went about their business, with white and pale gray adults squabbling with each other and with the brownish juveniles over precedents and places. With utter loathing Tikkisi knelt and fired both barrels into the closely packed birds, killing or maiming five of them. He reloaded and fired again, bringing two more gulls tumbling out of the sky, then again and again until the birds, grown wary of his power, flew out of range, circling and screaming at him. Then, with the loaded gun clutched fearfully and tightly, Tikkisi approached the thing at the tide line.

Yellow rain pants. Blue parka with hood up over the head. Boots gone. Life vest inflated. The body lay face upward, with the head and torso out of the water, and with only the flesh of face and hands exposed. The gulls had already been at it for an hour, for they had followed its face-down journey in the sea currents, and had been curious and frustrated until the body had stranded, and rolled over in the water when it had hung up on a rock. Now, the face was a horror, and around the flesh-stripped hands, thousands of gammaruses, the little shrimplike scavengers of the Arctic seas, clustered in moving gray gauntlets.

The scream came up from his belly and roared among the hills, and he fell to his knees, dropping the gun, hiding his own face in his hands. His body shuddered uncontrollably, and only barely did he cling to consciousness. God, god, why did he come back? Why had he returned to haunt and accuse? Tikkisi got up and steeled himself, tightening the muscles of his belly and chest. He would not be defeated. He would give this thing back to the sea. The tide still ebbed strongly enough to carry it out, and so taking courage, he waded into the water and tugged on the hood of the parka until it came free of the beach and the rocks and floated again.

Gammaruses left in thousands, swimming sideways to take refuge in the rocks on the bottom. Tikkisi pushed the body into deeper water until the current took it and carried it slowly away.

This place was cursed. Nanook, Bear-man, had come back from the sea for revenge and for his possessions, and the witches of the sky took unholy communion from his flesh. Tikkisi knew he could never again sleep, or relax attention in this place. He must be sure too that when he left, there would be no trail to follow, that no human eyes would watch him, and that he would offend no animal beings in his journeys. But first, the gulls.

With utter loathing he killed the injured birds and collected all of their bodies. He took them back to the camp and there hung them from guy ropes, having first disemboweled them and placed their stinking entrails on a rock. Soon ravens came, and this was good, for they would help him now and prevent the sky witches from betraying his path.

Tikkisi left, and behind him, in the battle-torn camp, the dead gulls fluttered their wings in a slight wind, as if in tortured flight, fluttering and turning, but getting nowhere.

In his first trip to carry equipment to the new camp, Tikkisi tried a trick he had used before with success. He tied a fishing lure and fifteen yards of line to his kayak paddle, just below the right-hand paddle blade. With each paddle stroke the lure dipped and followed, soon attracting a three-pound char, which struck and got itself hooked. Laughing, Tikkisi pulled it in and bit it through the head to kill it, giving thanks to the sea. He held the fish in his hands, admiring the spots on its flanks, red and orange jewels on metallic green, giving way to a sunset-pink and orange belly, touched with whitish yellow at the throat, and the pectoral and pelvic fins bordered with the purest white and edging orange and green. He admired, too, the rows of needle-sharp, backward-pointing teeth and the arrogant hook to the tip of the lower jaw.

"Fish, I see you, I see your bright colors and your strength. I know the great journeys in the sea world, and in the waters of stream and lake. Today I will taste you and your strength will be mine, and your body will become mine. Fish, I thank you."

He spoke this as an invocation, a prayer, and he used the language of the Inuit, and it made him feel good, and made the killing of a good creature less of an evil thing to have done, and this evidence of favor in the sight of the sea creatures cleared away the cloud of fear and depression that had followed him out of the other place.

He beached the kayak and unloaded, ready for portage, searching the sea first with binoculars to insure that nobody watched him. Before packing and carrying, however, he would build a fire and prepare the fish. He gathered driftwood and dwarf willow, with which he built a fire in a pit hollowed out in the shingle. As his billy boiled to make tea, he lashed stuff to his pack frame. It was low tide now, and long, twelve-inch-wide ribbons of kelp were exposed. Some of these he gathered. He cleaned the fish and wrapped it in kelp fronds, making a bundle. By this time the fire had died to coals, on which he laid his bundle, burying it then with coals and hot pebbles. He smoothed it over and hid the kayak, leaving the beach with no trace of his activities. The hard work of carrying up and over the dividing land to the south-facing bay would give him a great appetite, and by then the fish would be cooked, half baked, half steamed, in the kelp. He looked forward with great pleasure to the opening of the pit oven, when steam and delicious smells would come to him. As he sweated up the slope, he anticipated the steaming pink flesh, tender and flaked, and he would take some of the coal-crisped seaweed and sprinkle it on the fish, giving it a salty flavor. Then he would eat the kelp that had cooked closest to the fish in its fat and gravy. Life was good. After a few trips he could carry his kayak over the hill and be safe.

Whereas Tik had been torn in several directions, Tikkisi was not. He was serene and unhurried, and where before he had performed certain tasks with impatience and clumsiness, now, as Tikkisi, he performed each task with care and ritual, making it the most important thing in his life at that given moment. This care, this contemplation, and eventual stages of meditation, would give his senses a sharper edge. It was as if his inner self knew exactly how he must develop if he were to survive, although survival was not something Tikkisi worried at all about. Of his previous life in Britain, of the endless petty conflicts and hatreds of the summer, and of the final conflict that removed Philip the man from his life, Tikkisi remembered almost nothing. What he did remember was not in the form of accepted modern Anglo-Saxon reality, for although his surviving memories were vivid, many of them were dreamlike, and dreams that had come to him during that period came to be mingled without prejudice with the "reality" of actual happenings. His was a metamorphosis of the spirit, with Tik gone, and Tikkisi emerging as one of strength. The slate was wiped clean by shock and amnesia, and Richard Tavett, once known as Tik, had indeed become Tikkisi, but while Tik had always been searching for self, the thought that such a problem should even exist never crossed Tikkisi's mind. He was. He lived.

Once he had shifted over the stuff he needed from that place of evil, Tikkisi knew that he would have to work hard to store away food for even part of the winter. He had supplies from the old camp that might last two months. Therefore, with his gear safely hidden in the cave, Tikkisi turned his mind to hunting, first realizing that he would have to become truly familiar with his surroundings.

The cliffs behind the cave were the craggy, splintered brow of a dome-shaped hill, rising bare, devoid of vegetation, a landmark for sea travelers, and a burial place for the Inuit since ancient times. The passing of prehistoric glaciers had scarred it clearly, leaving marks which the old people said were made by the fingers of giants who had once played throwing games with the big erratic boulders that were stranded all over the place. Nowadays, many of the young, school-smart Inuit had begun to call the hill "the big tit," yet few cared to approach it, for deep inside, they still feared ghosts. The top of the hill was pimpled with twenty-three grave mounds, hollow, rock tombs of varying antiquity, each containing the remains of Inuit.

When Tikkisi saw the grave mounds, he felt not idle curiosity or morbid superstition, but rather a kind of relief from loneliness, for although all that remained of these people were whitened bones, scattered by foxes and gnawed by lemmings, they did constitute evidence of humanity, and besides, without knowing why, Tikkisi knew the names of everyone who lay here, even those whose bones had lain on this hill for hundreds of years. He stood in the approximate center of the burial place and raised his hand in greeting, speaking in Inuititut.

"Tikkisi greets you. He comes to live near you. He means you no ill. He will not desecrate your resting houses. Please give him your friendship and wisdom."

A flight of young loons flew below the cliffs, strengthening their wings for the coming journey south. They were early, and in them Tikkisi saw an omen, assuring him that things were well with the old people, that they did not resent his presence, and he saw too that they were advising him to prepare.

He sat down cross-legged among the stone mounds, closing his eyes and allowing his mind to dwell only on the flight of the loons. After twenty minutes he got up and walked over to one well-constructed cairn. One of the rocks had slipped off the roof struts of beluga ribs, and Tikkisi could peer down at a curled-up skeleton, intact but for a few of the small bones of the hands and feet that lemmings had dragged away. Lying beside the skeleton in this narrow, round space, was a soapstone lamp, fifteen inches long and eight inches wide, shaped like a section of an orange and made of soft, bluish green stone that had been blackened by ancient use. It was a stone of a type not found on the islands, and Tikkisi knew that it had seen long journeys, many snow houses and skin tents, and even the stone-and-whale-rib houses of the old Thule culture. This lamp had traveled long, and had been treated with great care. Apart from the lamp, there were a few bone needles, almost destroyed by time now, and the rusted remnants of an *ulu,* or curved woman's knife.

Tikkisi saw. He bent over the hole and whispered in.

"The sun lights you, Kila Umiapik, and I see you. Soon it will be winter. You know me. Be my friend."

He saw her as she had lain now for 107 years, and he saw too the procession of relatives, and the old lady being laid down, dressed in her finest eider-skin parka, with all her most precious things placed beside her, and he saw the men gathering stones from below, heavy slabs of rock that would deter even a bear. It had been spring, and the rocks still frozen to the ground, the men sweating with their labor, impatient to go and hunt, yet both sad and fearful at the passing of a woman of power. These islands had bred many people of power, most of them long forgotten now. Tikkisi could see it all, passing in his mind like a flash, and he felt no surprise, and questioned nothing.

He smiled and looked out toward the sea. Out there were hundreds of flightless eider ducks, easy hunting for a man with a kayak. He ran down the hill, rejoicing that this day was fairly calm.

✦ TEN ✦

Clyde, the anthropologist, stood outside the wheelhouse of the research vessel *Aivit* and scanned the shores with his binoculars. It was mid-September, and growing colder each day. Something was wrong, for the camp appeared deserted, and for some time. The skipper maneuvered the sturdy little ship through the mouth of the inlet and brought her to within a hundred yards of the shore, watching the depth sounder as he did so. He cut engines and nodded to one of the summer assistants, who went forward and released the anchor. The ship's oceanographer came on deck and stood beside Clyde.

"Where are those guys? I don't see a canoe. Do you reckon they're out hunting?"

"I don't think so. It doesn't look right. Let's go look." They launched the ship's dinghy and rowed across to the camp.

"Holy mackerel! What a mess! How can they leave a camp in this state?"

"Something is very wrong," said Clyde. "Phil always insisted on a neat camp, and it was never like this. I don't think they left it in this state."

He searched around in the wreckage of the cook tent and picked up a can of evaporated milk that had been opened. He sniffed it. "This camp has been deserted for weeks. Let's see if we can find a note or something."

The oceanographer went into Philip's tent and came out with his logbook. "Clyde, look here! The last entry in this book was made by Philip on August sixth. That's five weeks ago."

They read the last entry in the black, imitation leather book, written in Philip's precise, neat lettering, always done with black waterproof ink.

August 6, 1958:
There is every evidence of a coming storm, and I must bring forward my plans by a couple of days in order to compensate for a potential loss of time. This morning I intend to go out across the bay to scout for a temporary camp on one of the islands. It will probably be wet and cold.

The rest of the page was blank, and obviously Philip had intended to write more. Clyde was leafing backward through the logbook when the oceanographer nudged him.

"We've got visitors."

Joe and Neviaksi were sweating from having traveled so fast. Solemnly they shook hands and exchanged greetings. Neviaksi said that they had observed the approach of the ship and guessed it would come here, so accordingly he and Joe had hurried overland to meet them. They had walked a long distance. Clyde waited patiently for the story to unfold, translating it in a condensed form for the other white man.

It was wind and foxes, they said, and not the Inuit, who had broken this camp. The two other white men, the big man and the boy, had not lived here for over a month. The boat, the kayak, one tent and many other things were gone. Neviaksi knew what was missing because he had been in the camp himself, and his older brother Ipeelee had spent many days here while Joe and Neviaksi had gone north with Ooniak to hunt walrus. Many things were gone from the camp, and many things left. Neviaksi then told them of how he and Noah had been hunting in their kayaks, and had found a body on the shore. He told too of how he had found burnt pieces of a freighter canoe, and one charred thing that the white man used to carry in the canoe, a thing like this. Neviaksi pointed to the oceanographer's life jacket. He continued to describe how he and Noah had pulled the body out of the water and built a cairn over it because of the birds. They had searched the shores where current came in, but had found nothing else. Noah, who owned a bible written in syllabics, remembered some prayers and had said them, and they both sang a hymn, but they were afraid that this was not enough, and they hoped that the other white men could have the proper prayers said for him. Clyde asked whose body it was. Neviaksi answered that it was the body of the big white man with yellow hair, but the body was not pleasant to look upon. He made a face.

Clyde turned to the oceanographer. "It looks as if they've drowned, burnt their canoe under them." He shook his head. "You know, I warned that silly limey not to smoke in the canoe when fiddling with gas. Bet you any money that was what did it."

"Maybe one white man not drowned," said Joe in his stilted English.

"Where is he then, Joe?"

Neviaksi glared at the younger man, who looked down at his boots. "Gone," said Joe.

"Gone where?"

"Gone," said Joe again. "Not come back." Then he thought. "Maybe he dead too. Eskimo man no find kayak. White boy very good kayak man." He smiled. "Maybe white boy dead in water too."

"Come on," said the oceanographer. "We have got to report this to the Mounties right away. We can get them on the radio." The four men went over to the *Aivit* in the dinghy, and as he rowed, Clyde wondered who would tell Philip's wife.

For five days, low-flying aircraft flew search patterns over the area, even though the RCMP and the local air force base commander did not really think they would find anything. An RCMP "Beaver" risked a dangerous landing to take Philip's body to Whaler's Bay, whence it was flown out to Montreal in a sealed casket. The RCMP sergeant from Whaler's Bay collected personal effects from the camp, and noted the two shot holes in one of the tents, entering that fact as well as excerpts from Philip's log into a confidential report to his superiors in G Division. He and his special constable dismantled the remaining tents and packed the scattered gear into boxes to be consolidated into one cache, which they then covered with a tarpaulin and weighted down with rocks. He took inventory of everything, and removed only those things which were obviously Philip's and Tik's personal effects. There was no space on the plane to take out everything, and the university could make up its own mind if it wanted the gear brought out or not.

Investigations revealed that a tent, sleeping bags, camping equipment, tools, weapons, and ammunition were missing, and it was presumed that these had been taken for the temporary camp that Philip had written about. It all seemed to indicate that both men were lost in the storm that had raged over the period immediately following the last entry in the logbook, but after visiting the camp, the sergeant had a gut feeling that something was amiss. There were too many unanswered questions. Why the shot holes in the tent? Why did they take things like snowshoes and a pair of army-style cross-country skis? Why did they empty their case of twelve-gauge and .22 ammunition and leave so much .270 ammunition? And how was it that this biologist, who had the usual licenses and so forth, didn't know the game laws about killing gulls? Hell, there were dead gulls all over the place. Also, the Britisher's log hinted at some hostility between the two men, not so unusual in an isolated camp like this, but worthy of note. He would remember to question old Ipeelee when he came into Whaler's Bay to stock up on supplies and sell his skins. Where on earth was the second body? Of course, it was easy to overlook a body, or for it to sink, but the sergeant was disturbed by garbled rumors in the settlement that the young white man was some kind of shaman. He decided that he would have to keep an even closer ear to the local grapevine in the coming winter months.

While the planes searched overhead, Tikkisi stayed hidden in his cave, with his kayak pulled up out of sight. He was fervently thankful that there was still no snow on the ground to betray him with tracks. During the five days of hiding, he made good use of his time by building dry stone walls inside the cave, to close off a living space. He built double walls, filling the space between with moss. He also built a sleeping platform, with moss on the ground, covered then with canvas, then covered with a mattress he made from some of Philip's sleeping-bag sheets (Philip could never bear the thought of sleeping in a dirty bag) and filled with eiderdown from the hundreds of vacated nests. Over that he laid a foam rubber mattress and his own caribou-hide sleeping robe. With all this and two down-filled sleeping bags, he would be warm and comfortable no matter how cold it got outside.

He now had a small room, roofed by the cave, with sleeping

area and cooking area separated by a piece of tarpaulin that could be tied up or let down as he wished. Besides the living and sleeping area, he also had enough cave space to give him a storeroom, protected by rocks to keep out the foxes. His sleeping area was small enough to be considerably warmed by the hurricane lamp, which used very little fuel.

By the time the *Aivit* came, Tikkisi had stocked up with a hundred thirty ducks and guillemots, all of which he had skinned, split, salted and dried. He had also dried fillets from over two hundred fish, caught in his nets during days too rough for kayak hunting. Calm weather was now becoming the exception. He had also managed to kill four small ringed seals, the blubber and meat of which would be an invaluable addition to his food supplies, for the flesh of fish and fowl was not adequate to keep a man strong. However, a mere four seals was far too little, and days calm enough for seal hunting were becoming fewer and fewer. Those supplies he had taken from the other camp would have to be rationed, and things like tea, sugar and flour must become occasional treats instead of staples. Still, he worried about nothing, for each day was busy and joyful, and six weeks of hunting, kayaking, fishing, walking, berry gathering, doing the many jobs necessary for life made him fitter and stronger than ever.

In his previous, now buried life, there had been many things he would have liked to have done, but which he had not done because they might seem strange, different, or illogical. But now Tikkisi did always what he wanted to do, or what he deemed necessary. Right up until the waters froze in October, he cleansed himself in a nearby stream, naked and gasping with cold, but feeling tremendously exhilarated afterward, with his skin tingling like fire. He now invented exercises that would enable him to endure cramp and cold in the kayak, to relax, to breathe easily. He imitated the movements of birds, fish and seals, and created mind-poems to go along with them. Tikkisi was filled with the need to become a part of everything, and in these daily rituals, some of them Inuit, but most of them his own, he sought to further this ideal. He would become invisible, indivisible, inviolate, a part of all things. He made songs — songs for walking, songs for paddling, songs for pulling nets, songs for calling seals, songs for scraping skins, and after a while he could make the songs run through his head and grow without having to be vocalized. For each creature he killed, he had a ritual to recognize it, and he never ate any creature without first thanking the souls of those whose tissues he took into his own body. And there was not waste in any of this, for it helped heal his mind, and make him strong, and at peace.

The air search was called to a halt due to bad weather, and news of the loss of the two would-be Arctic explorers reached newspapers in southern Canada and England. Tik's mother had a nervous breakdown, but refused to believe her son was dead, and wrote letter after letter to the Canadian embassy in London, to the university, to the Arctic Institute, all of them begging that searches be continued. For the most part, the letters were answered sympathetically, and forgotten.

Philip's wife moved out to British Columbia to live with her mother.

In the Beaker Islands, Tikkisi was beleaguered for two weeks with rain, sleet, snow and winds. Kayak hunting was impossible, and everything else difficult. Geese gathered, waiting for the weather to clear before heading south.

When the weather finally broke, Tikkisi gave thanks to the sky god and took his .22 rifle, harpoon, line and float and went out in the kayak for two days. He got nothing at all, and was forced to live on bannock and dried fish. Finally realizing that he was in the wrong time and place, he decided to head back to his cave, and meditate for a day, and fast, and try to reach out in his mind for the secret places of the animals he hunted. On the way back to his den, he passed a long, sloping shell beach. The beach was only half a mile or so from the cave, and indeed, Tikkisi had already carried loads of crushed shell from the place to cover the floor of his home. His arms were aching from the strain of paddling against the current, and he grunted out a chanting song, feeling the last reserves of strength flowing into his hands, wrists, forearms, upper arms, shoulders, and back, from the furnace of his belly. Spray wet his face, tasting of salt. Then he saw the silvery plumes of whale breath, and felt joy that he had been pulled homeward, to greet the sea brothers who surely must have discovered that he lived here now. It was some minutes before he spotted the tall fin of the leader, and he hooted and yodeled and would have stopped paddling if current and waves had permitted him. First one fin, then another, turned toward him. Two hundred yards away from Tikkisi in his kayak, two killer whales stood in the water, thrashing their powerful tails to keep heads and bodies up above the choppy, gray surface of the sea, their massive bulk supported as far as their pectoral fins out of the water. Tikkisi gave a shrill whistle, and seemingly satisfied, the whales sank back into the water, and one, a young female with a backward-curving dorsal fin, began to porpoise toward him, showing her back and the black and white markings clearly. When she reached the kayak she splattered Tikkisi with water from her tail, and he laughed, and had to paddle hard to keep upright. He felt no fear. The other whales, all six, followed and began to circle the kayak. Whale breath hung in the air and filled his nostrils with its vitality. They circled continuously, like a whirlpool moving across the surface of the sea, giving the kayak more space in front than behind, as if they were edging it toward the beach. Tikkisi had little choice as to where he should paddle, and he followed their movement. Then he saw the shapes of nine beluga, seven adults and two young, beached in the shallow waves. Understanding now, he paddled hard to the beach and landed.

The largest of the stranded animals was a male, and although it was still living, its left pectoral fin had been cruelly torn, and bled profusely. The tail had also been bitten, leaving several long scars ending in a ragged wound where the tip of one fluke had been ripped off by the teeth of the killer whale. Tikkisi waded in knee-deep water and crouched down by the beluga's head, looking into the eye that observed him, an eye set like a pebble in a head of smooth white marble.

"I see you, brother; I feel your pain." He stroked the domed head and felt the now feeble puff of warm, moist air through the blowhole. Oh, but this creature had known such terror and desperation! Had it thought that this smooth beach led to safety and escape? Had it been confused? Or had it preferred this form of suicide to death at the jaws of the sea hunters? Tears came to Tikkisi's eyes.

"What can I do?" he asked the whale, looking back at the leisurely cruising black triangles offshore. Would they accept the life of just one beluga? The stranded beluga whistled and raspberried feebly to each other, and Tikkisi asked himself if he should kill this one dying bull, and if so, how he should do it. In the creature's eye he saw acceptance, and he thought he even saw trust. But no, surely it was not for him to kill, he must return the whale to the sea. He struggled with the smooth body and managed to get it into three feet of water, getting himself soaked in the process, but with a few strokes of the injured tail, the beluga pushed itself back onto the beach. Cold numbed Tikkisi's legs, and he got stiffly out of the water again.

"It is better that you should return to the sea and feed other whales, better that than to die on the beach here." He waded back into the water again, trying now to get two young into the water, but they too beached themselves again. Could it be that the calls of the injured bull drew them to their own deaths? Or were they also terrified of the hunting cries of the killer whales? Should Tikkisi then end the agonies of the bull, and try to return the others to the sea? He made a decision and went over to his kayak to fetch the harpoon.

Gripping the shaft with both hands, he stood to one side of the animal.

"Forgive me, little brother," he said, first in English, and then in the Inuit language. "May your spirit return to the sea!" And with a yell, he thrust hard and leaned with all his weight on the shaft until the steel head reached the beluga's heart. Blood fountained out of the blowhole and its eyes glazed in death. The vividness of the scarlet blood on the pure white of the whale's skin was dramatically beautiful, but Tikkisi could not bear to look. He rushed around to the other animals and with both hands splashed sea water over them to wash off the blood, but the sea around became opaquely red.

It took fifteen minutes to cut out the harpoon head, to roll the body to deeper water and to fasten a short length of line to it. Tikkisi then had to paddle hard and fast in order to tow the animal out, for it kept sinking at the head, releasing blood and bubbles of air from the wound in the side. Ten minutes of hard paddling brought it into six feet of water, and Tikkisi's arms were burning with fatigue. Finally, he leaned forward on his paddle, physically and emotionally drained.

The big bull killer whale approached the kayak slowly, and with extreme caution. Tikkisi slashed the towing line and the killer whale took the dead beluga by one flipper and towed it

163

with ease out into deeper water. The rest of the pod followed him, and soon they were gone. Tikkisi headed slowly back to shore. It began to snow.

For two hours he struggled to return the eight remaining beluga to the sea, but now they were all too well stranded, and all he was succeeding in doing was causing them distress. He got the smaller gray ones into the water at least a dozen times, but always they drove themselves back onto the beach. Finally he walked wooden legged out of the water and collapsed. His teeth chattered. Fire. He needed fire and hot liquid to replace some of the heat he had lost. With an armful of a dry, oily shrub, he lit a blaze and piled on driftwood that was scattered along the beach. He always carried tea and a billy in the kayak, and in a waterproof bag he kept spare pants, socks, and a shirt. Shivering, he stripped, slapping the blue-tinged skin until it became red. Warm clothing was sheer ecstasy, and already the billy was beginning to bubble.

All the time he had been taking care of his own needs, he had been talking in a soft voice to the beluga, telling them of each of his actions and its significance. Being creatures of the sea, they might not have understood, and been afraid. Part of him told him that what he was doing was nonsense, but then, building a fire outside was nonsense too, for he was so close to his own camp. Yet Tikkisi could not leave the animals to die alone like this, out of their element. Flakes of snow fell and disappeared in the heating stones, and his wet clothing, spread over rocks by the fire, began to steam. The whales wheezed in shallow and irregular breaths. Death was just a matter of time.

Tikkisi began to conduct an inquisition within himself, endeavoring to determine whether or not he had been correct in ending the life of the old beluga. He asked himself if the leader of the killer whales had exerted power over him, urging him to bring his quarry back from the land, and he sensed an immensely important drama between the two species of Cetacea. The whole of this inquiry he held verbally, out loud, as if asking the eight beluga still on the beach to comment. Sitting cross-legged in front of the fire, he drank the hot tea from his battered enamel mug, blessing the warmth it carried to his belly. Now his legs and feet were tingling as if on fire, and he felt light headed. As he delved deeper into his thoughts and reasons for his actions, pain suddenly blurred Tikkisi's inner vision. Upon the repeating memory loop of the death thrust to the heart of the beluga, nightmarish images intruded, pushing more and more clearly into his actual vision until blurred and hideous things seemed about to come lurching out of the gloom and the snow to reach him, hurt him. He jumped to his feet and seized the harpoon, turned his back to the sea and stood there.

"No!" He screamed, and with his defiance of those fearful things, the images switched off so abruptly that the wheezing of the beluga and the hiss and crackle of the fire seemed to jump into an amplified clarity. His heart pounded.

A thought, a fitful hope, came to him that perhaps the beluga could survive until the next tide, twelve hours hence, and that then the rising waters would lift them off. Then, with the hunting pack gone, they could be directed to safety. Which of the animals was the leader now?

"Is it you?" he asked of one female, touching her gently by the folds that hid the nipples on either side of her vagina. He ran his hand over her fine smoothness, over her belly, knowing that she was swollen with thick milk. "Do you not wish this one, this little gray one, to grow large and strong in the sea? Please live, little sister, please live, and show the others."

One by one and collectively he talked to the sea people, joking and pleading, trying to comfort them with his touch and his voice, hoping that they would live.

In the periphery of his vision the flames danced, and as he moved among the still forms on the beach, the words and melody of a tongue perhaps even as ancient as that of the Inuit came back to him, and he began to sing an old Welsh lullaby which a long-ago grandmother had sung to him in another plane. The song came dancing with the flames into his mind, as though demanding to be translated into sound. And then the lilting, sibilant words came softly to his mouth, and he sang with great beauty.

For twelve hours he stayed with the beluga, all through the night, until dawn came and slanted light on a world covered with snow, until all of the driftwood turned to ash, and until the last beluga died before the returning waves lapped at its tail flukes. Tikkisi returned to his cave and slept a deep, deep sleep.

When he awoke, he ate heartily and returned to the beach, finding the dead beluga, all eight of them, still lying there. He knew now what he must do.

ELEVEN

Tikkisi lowered the square chunk of *muktuk* into the grave cairn and stepped back. It was not that he thought that this muddle of dried human bones would have any use for such a delicacy, but he was sure that the spirit of the old woman would be aware of his thoughts and appreciate this ritual gesture.

"Old one, I thank you for your wisdom."

He had no doubt that it was Kila Umiapik who had cleared his mind as he slept, allowing him to wake with plans for the butchering of the dead whales, and for the caching of the meat and blubber, more than enough to last the winter. He gave thanks also to the creatures of the sea, and after the long and arduous task of butchering the animals and building the big stone cache, Tikkisi had taken the eight hearts, paddled out to deep water, and dropped them into the sea.

"Old one," said Tikkisi, "the birds are going. It will be quiet. Will I be lonely?"

He sighed and stood there like a statue against the skyline. In the distance, snow flurries moved like stalking beasts across the surface of the sea, and now only a part of the recent snow-falls melted off during the day. There was a chill in the air, a silence that seemed to be growing, a silence that was seized and stretched by the very noisiness of the flocks of ducks and mergansers that still dallied in the odd, sheltered bay. In strings and Vs the geese winged south, honking as they passed . . . we leave . . . we leave . . . we leave. . . .

Shallow ponds were already filmed with ice, and the dark, hanging cloud bellies were pregnant with snow. Tikkisi had many things to do: he must collect all the driftwood he could find, and he must make an Inuit-style stove from the top of an empty steel fuel drum. He would make a trip to the old campsite and salvage odds and ends — there was a second pair of army-type cross-country skis there, and he could use them to make runners for a little toboggan for man-hauling. He picked his way down the hill, sniffing the air. He must leave now, before the weather worsened.

At the campsite on the inlet, Tikkisi had expected to feel terror, but he felt only a desolation of the spirit. Memories of the summer, especially of the good times, flashed through his mind, but when he tried to capture and examine these memories, they eluded him. The memory images of Philip were the vaguest of all, and he loomed huge, dreamlike, faceless, a darkling giant haloed with blond hair.

Now that the camp itself was gone, the rows of rocks that they had used to anchor the guy lines looked like the remnants of some strange game. There, the canvas-covered mound of stuff, there, the marks of the fireplace where he used to burn garbage. He stood in the center of the site, trying to reconstruct in his mind the way it had been before, trying to fill it with personalities. Only old Ipeelee was clear, and Tikkisi could visualize his face and hear his voice, see the stubby, gnarled fingers working dexterously on a carving. He couldn't see

Philip, though, and he couldn't see himself as he had been —
Tik, the shackled idiot, coward, crybaby. He spoke aloud to
this deserted place.

"I am Tikkisi, brother to the sea people." But as he made this
proclamation, the nature of the English word "I" intruded and
bothered him, and made no sense, so he repeated the proclamation, making it feel better without the "I."

"Tikkisi, brother to the sea people, is here."

Neither his childhood, nor his coming to this place with
Philip was clear, and even the effort of thought in this area
caused him distress. Memories of his first expedition seemed
clear enough, but they too were hedged with nothingness,
with no before-time, no after-time, no between-time.

"Surely," he thought, "Tikkisi must be a nothingness, a
spirit in a human body, for he has no affiliations with humans.
He is alone." He thought again and said to himself, "I am
afraid of other people." But it didn't make sense, because he
knew so many things. The amnesia had been selective, leaving
him knowledge, but taking away faces and feelings of so much
that was prior to his Arctic experience. He felt dizzy and sat
down. He must calm his mind, not allow it to torture him.

He closed his eyes and began to count his breaths, and to
watch the spreading and receding of colors in the blackness behind his eyelids. Visions grew and a thousand breaths passed,
two thousand, three, and Tikkisi thought that once again he
had fought within himself a contest between the spirits of the
sea, of the air, and of the land; that he had been torn between
them, destroyed, and reborn; that he had once again defeated
Bear-man and thrown him to the sea people. But still, Bear-
man was always a danger, reappearing, and he, Tikkisi, must
be wary and cunning. He must avoid other humans. His only
true friends were the good spirits of the earth and sea. He
shivered. So many friends were leaving the land now. Soon

the sea would freeze over and close him out from the creatures
of the sea with a ceiling of ice. He would walk on the roof.
Would they hear his footsteps?

He stretched his limbs and got up to rummage through the
pile of stuff, finding a length of wire, some nails, pieces of
cord, the extra pair of skis. Then he began to work on an
empty forty-five-gallon drum, cutting off the top third with a
cold chisel so that he would end up with something that looked
like a basin, twelve inches deep. He could convert this to an
excellent little stove, modeled on stoves found in tents and
shacks all over the Eastern Arctic, a stove that would burn anything, and that could be used for heating and cooking.

Tikkisi had become accustomed to loneliness, and as he
clanged and banged and boomed on the steel drum, he began
to sing in time to the noise. It was getting dark, and he wanted
to finish, so he worked with a fury, hollering and whooping a
work song, making up words as he went along. Forgetting
caution, and not believing that anybody could be within several miles, he made sounds that shook the hills.

Noah had been hunting hares and setting a few fox traps.
He came to the brow of the ridge and was considering going
down to the campsite and borrowing the tarpaulin, to sleep
for a few hours beneath it before trekking home. The sounds
that reached him were at first faint, and Noah thought it might
be a late flock of geese, but on reaching the highest point of
land, the banging and chanting assaulted his ears, and memories of his childhood reached out at him, when Ipeelee's
father, an *angakok* of some repute, had called the camps in the
north of the islands. He had caused them to build a large snow
house, such as they sometimes held dances in, and made them
sit around in a circle, and had worn a terrifying mask, and had

spoken in words which he and Neviaksi, his cousin, had not understood . . . strange, old words. Yes, and Ipeelee, who was fifteen years older than he and Neviaksi, had whispered to them, both small and terrified boys, "He says he will fly to the moon, and there he will talk with a wise man, and bring back news of the hunters there." Aieee! Then the *angakok* ordered them to close their eyes, saying that they would die if they looked, and the air in the big igloo had moaned and thrummed and whistled over their heads, while the *angakok* sang in a voice that became more and more distant as he flew away. That was before the white shaman came, the missionary from the settlement, who had insisted that the old magic was evil, and the songs of the old ones full of devils.

Indeed, Noah was a converted Christian, but the missionary could never fly to the moon, or see through the eyes of birds, or cause death to an enemy by creating in his belly a *tupilak* — a terrifying spirit that would eat the soul. Now, as Noah looked down, he could see nothing in the shadows, he could only hear the ghostly chanting and drumming, and he caught words that were partly Inuit, and partly of other languages. He had little doubt that he was hearing a ghost. This was the camp of the one they called Nanook, who had died, and of the young one who went from the earth without a trace. Noah said a quick prayer and headed homeward, walking all through the night.

When Tikkisi finished cutting, he loaded his kayak and headed back to the mouth of the Inlet where the *Aivit* had left a cache of fuel, equipment, and supplies for research parties that were due to fly into the Beaker Islands the following spring. To his delight, Tikkisi found several sections of stove pipe, of which he borrowed four. Then, with the currents to help him, he left, noting that the salt water was freezing around rocks and around the splash guards of his paddles.

By noon the next day, four inches of snow had fallen, and air temperatures were well below freezing. The small lakes were all filmed with ice, some of them with enough ice to permit travel. Neviaksi hitched a small team of six dogs to his smallest *komatik* and headed for the white man's old campsite. Noah had been reluctant to accompany him, but Joe came willingly. As much as any sensible hunter, Neviaksi was wary of offending spirits or demons, but he had strong suspicions that the disappearance of the young white man was not what it seemed to be. He had a hunter's perception, recognizing and registering a thousand items of information, sifting them unconsciously to form solutions which came to him as "knowing." Neviaksi's assumptions were not based on formal logic, but rather on multiplaned patterns of awareness that seemed to him so simple and obvious that a man never had to argue points.

On reaching the site, Neviaksi immediately saw the remnants of the cut drum, and knew exactly what it meant. "The white boy lives," he said.

Joe nodded. "Truly, this may be so, but where is he?"

"He travels by kayak, two days, perhaps three. He intends to camp through the winter and hide from us. We must watch for him."

"Hah! A white man cannot survive!" said Joe scornfully. He paused. "Why did he not return with the others, in the ship?" He paused again, as if considering his own question. "He fears the other white men! Could it be that he killed the big man? The police searched for him, did they not?"

Neviaksi shook his head. His brother, Ipeelee, had told him

that the boy had a good spirit, and Neviaksi did not believe that such a one would commit murder.

"This man and Noah, we saw the body of the big man, and it had no signs of knife, bullet or spear. He was too strong for the boy to kill without a weapon. He died of fire and sea. We only know that the boy lives, and that he hides."

Joe spoke hotly. "He is a white man, and they are strange and violent, and they kill and fight for pleasure. I have seen this. The white man will grow hungry, and if he does not die he will seek us out and try to take our food. Perhaps he will try to kill us. A man must keep a rifle in easy reach on a sled this winter."

Shocked at Joe's words, Neviaksi shook his head. "Our camp has food enough for him, and if he comes we will feed him as we feed all travelers. However, that one will not seek us out, and he will not try to kill us. If he lives, then the other white men will search until they find him." He stopped, half remembering something Ipeelee had said to him. "If we tell them, they will search."

Joe looked out from the frosted oval of his parka hood. "We will tell them?"

"When they come to ask us, we will tell them."

"This man believes the white man will die," said Joe.

"This man thinks different," countered Neviaksi.

Noah kept his own counsel. Neither Joe nor Neviaksi had heard those sounds, and if it were indeed that the boy Tikkisi had returned, then he had returned from the sea, from the land of dead souls, and he would be searching for a body to dwell in. Perhaps, thought Noah, a man should name a new puppy Tikkisi, just in case? But that probably would not be enough, for such a one as he would not be content to dwell within the body of a dog. It all made sense though, for they had found the body of the big one and had conducted rituals for him, but for the other, who had such close brotherhood to the sea creatures, they had conducted no rituals, neither white nor Inuit. It was obvious that such a one would return and roar his anger and give vent to magical sounds. Noah determined, whatever the others decided, to do nothing that might offend the spirit of the one they called Tikkisi, Boy-who-smiles.

As winter strengthened its grip on the land, there followed weeks of high winds and driving snow. Like a hibernating bear, Tikkisi retreated into his cave and stayed there. The drifts built up in walls of densely packed snow, sealing the cave even further, leaving only a curved tunnel, which he dug out, and a chimney through the crevice where smoke and gases passed from his stove. Snug and silent inside the den, he could hear nothing of the winds that raged and whined outside. The heat and yellow light of the hurricane lamp kept the den warm enough, and if he burned driftwood and blubber in the barrel-top stove, it would become unbearably hot, causing him to strip to the waist and squat there, gleaming with sweat while he cooked his food or melted snow for water to drink.

During the short hours of daylight, he ventured outside briefly to pass body wastes, but the weather invariably drove him back in. For one month he stayed almost entirely in the den, allowing himself to be transported in and out of sleep, a sleep filled with dreams.

The tasks he performed were simple, for he had stored plenty of food in the cave, and snow provided water. Soon, he began to grow impatient with his hours of waking, and sought to continue the voyages and adventures of the dream worlds. He would spend hours in a straight-backed, cross-legged position, humming to himself and staring at the light of the hurricane lamp or at the red eye of the air vent of the stove. Soon, his dreams began to invade wakefulness, and he found that he could direct them, populate his cave with colors, sounds, creatures — or, if he wished, he could leave his body and fly out over a changed world. At times he would allow the lamp to burn out, so that he sat or lay in utter silence and utter darkness, a darkness that he could gradually fill with visions of fantastic, fluid colors.

In one such waking dream, Kila Umiapik came down from the hill to talk with him. They spoke together in a magical tongue, neither English nor Welsh nor Inuit, yet they both understood clearly. Tikkisi related all that he had experienced to her, illustrating his stories by painting vividly colored thought images on the stone walls, showing her his life as he knew it, the great battle he had fought with the Bear-man and with the witches of the sky, and he told too of his communications with the creatures of the sea, and the long voyages on which they guided him. She listened with wisdom to all that he had to say, adding sometimes to his tales with images of her own, and she sat there, old and bent, enveloped in her bird-skin parka. Tikkisi boasted aloud, "You see, old one, I have shelter, food, water, heat — everything that I need."

She answered him. "Man-boy, are you sure that this is all you have need of?" and he caught his breath, seeing an almost predatory glint in her eye. She knew, she knew! He should never have invited her to come down here! He tried to stop his mind from darting to the old one's thighs, but she caught his mind and pulled it there, to those old, thin thighs, covered with furs. Her laughter filled the cave.

"You want! Man-boy, admit your want!"

With revulsion he shook his head, but she laughed again and pulled the parka over her head. She stripped off the inner parka of soft fawnskin and stretched thin arms to him, and he stared at those thin, leathery dugs, hanging like small empty

pouches against her rib cage. He backed up against the wall.
No . . . no . . . no . . . no. . . . She laughed and began
to change, growing first fatter, fuller, then younger, and the
old breasts were filling and lifting, the arms becoming more
rounded, the skin drawing tight and glossy over the cheek
bones, eyes becoming brighter, wrinkles vanishing. And then
she smiled, and as she did so her eyes, hard before, took on a
softness that caused her to look like Annie . . . yes, she was
Annie, but not Annie, and her smiled filled the cave with
summer. Come to me, come to me, come to me. Now she was
a young and beautiful woman, half naked. She was beckoning,
taunting, pleading, and he began to sweat beneath his clothing.
Come to me, come to me. He tore off his own parka, the
sweater, the shirt, and he took her in his arms and felt the taut
buds of nipples against his chest. Come to me, come to me.
She reached for him and he lay stripped, and they coupled
in urgent frenzy on the sleeping platform, and outside, un-
heard, the wind hurried and moaned through the rocks.

A hundred miles and more away, Annie moaned in her sleep
then came awake at the sound of her own voice. Her throat
was dry and she wanted a drink of cold water from the pot by
the stove. She got up and crouched by the stove, shivering a
little. Her grandfather came and stood beside her, placing his
hand on her shoulder.

"You gave voice in your dream, little daughter," he said.

"Yes," she said, with a sharp intake of breath as the dream
thrust into her wakefulness.

"He reaches you?"

Suddenly embarrassed, she nodded, and a tear rolled down
her face, making her conscious of other moist places in her
body. Her grandfather crouched beside her, speaking in a low

voice so as not to wake the others, who snored softly beneath their caribou-skin robes.

"Now is the time of darkness for him. Now is the time of testing," said Ipeelee. "He wishes you no harm, but holds you in great esteem. Do not fear him. Now he will either grow strong and gain wisdom, or he will go out into the darkness and die once again. Either way, no harm will come to you."

"But this foolish one does not wish for him to push into her dreams!" said Annie.

Ipeelee laughed softly and touched the string on which there hung a small pouch, down under her undershirt, between her breasts. It contained a small carving of a loon.

"Ah, is that true?" he asked, then smoothed her hair, as he had done so many times when she was a child. "Sleep, little one, it is over."

And as she returned to her bed, Ipeelee took another piece of driftwood and put it into the stove, nodding to himself as he did so. . . .

Tikkisi's mind snapped back to reality and he found that he was truly naked in the darkness, and alone, totally alone.

"Oh, god, no!" He fumbled for matches to light the lamp. The place smelled of his own body. He dressed, feeling shame.

Outside, the wind was beginning to die, and the aurora writhed overhead like eels in a bowl. He walked up to the top of the burial hill and enjoyed the bite of wind in his face. He stopped beside the old woman's grave cairn.

"Old one, do not let me trick myself. That is the way to madness."

Now, as he stood there, he could hardly believe the wealth of sensations and sexual ecstasy which his under-mind had provided for his sensation-starved consciousness. But he under-

177

stood what it meant. He did not have the strength to live the life of a monk in a cell. No, he must travel, explore, hunt, fish through the ice, make things, fill his waking hours with real sensations and not allow the worlds of dreams and other-place to capture his spirit. Whispering, he spoke to the mound of stones.

"Old one, I understand now."

As he reached the entrance of his den, something darted out of the snow tunnel. It was a fox. Tikkisi cried out with delight at its delicate and nimble movements, at its white, toy-like fluffiness. He made noises at it, but it ran off and stopped a distance away from him, curious, but still poised and ready for flight. Tikkisi went inside and came out with a piece of partially frozen boiled whale meat. He put the tidbit by the entrance.

"You and I must become friends," he said.

A rosy wash was tinting the southeastern sky.

178

⤙ TWELVE ⤙

The little fish came wriggling out of the ice hole and was laid on the snow. Feeling then its mute agony and imagining its fury, Tikkisi hastened to end this with a swift chop of his hunting knife. Watery red on trampled snow. Gills like flames in silver. The pale yellow lamplight was reflected and magnified by the dome of the igloo, and the hole in the floor was a black eye to another world. As fishes passed into or through the small column of lighter water, he could see them, but outside of that column they were invisible. A skim of ice formed on the top and he swept it aside. The hole had been open for a month now, and its sides were smooth and rounded with new ice. In another month or so he would have to cut a new hole. He lowered the lure into the water again and watched fish make passes at it. There was something about fishing with a lure that smacked of trickery, and although he enjoyed it, he felt it to be a somewhat perverse activity, tinged wtih deceit.

In this lake there was one big fish that he had been trying to catch since the first day he had dug the hole and built the snow house over it. The fish was a large-headed, evil-jawed female whose ovaries had long since atrophied and whose gills were pallid with parasitic crustacea. She was an elusive old cannibal, twenty or thirty years old, and it seemed to Tikkisi that she was the guardian of the lake, always shunning his hooks and always insuring that no more than nine of the smaller fish got caught. Nine. Magic number. When larger numbers of fish began attacking the baited lure in a feeding frenzy, she too was aroused, and would dart and devour her own kind, scaring them away from the column of light and from the scents of food and fresh fish blood.

Water was heating in a billy over the little gasoline stove. Outside on the ski-runner sled, Tikkisi had brought a chunk of bannock, some salt, a square of frozen whale meat and blubber, a piece of canvas, a caribou skin and one sleeping bag. He would eat and sleep here before making a trek to another, larger lake where the fishing was better and where he had cut another fishing hole and built a larger, higher snow house over it.

The inside of these fishing-hole snow houses was always considerably warmer than the outside, for the water holes gave off heat, which was trapped in the domes. Feathery crystals of frozen vapor hung from the walls and receded before the fiercer heat of the little, roaring, gasoline stove. Tikkisi was relaxed, looking forward to the meal of fresh, boiled fish. He looked down into the hole and saw the magnified body of the great she-fish as it swirled past the lure.

He laughed. Enough for today. He went outside and brought in a chunk of whale meat and blubber. He chopped a piece off and popped it into his mouth, chewing and tasting the raw, cold sweetness of it. The meat, blubber and saliva made a paste in his mouth, and this he spat into the ice hole, watching as it spread into a pinkish cloud of particles, slowly descending in the water. Excited fish darted into the light, snatching at the food, and the big she-fish at them.

"Fish, you see how I share with you food from the sea? Can you taste the sea? Or have you been locked in this lake for too many ages to remember?"

He chewed up more meat and fat and spat that into the hole too, drawing more fish. The old cannibal gobbled a fingerling, and others scattered, leaving only their bigger, bolder relatives. Without the rich marine food, these fish took a long time to grow and spawned while still small, but although their flesh was not as fat or juicy as sea-run char, they still provided a welcome change from frozen fish or meat.

Tikkisi rolled up the line and put it and the lure away in a pouch he carried on his belt. He pegged up the small square of canvas that formed the door to the igloo and looked outside into the darkness. Light from the door caught the twin yellow jewels of two pairs of eyes, and Tikkisi whistled softly. The male fox came forward first and caught the fish head that Tikkisi tossed to him. The female approached more cautiously, but she would be the first to take a tidbit from his hand, so Tikkisi squatted patiently, speaking softly, extending the head and guts of another fish until she came to the doorway and took it. He had been feeding them for a month now, and they were no longer afraid of him, sometimes even permitting him to touch the wonderful fluffy softness of their white fur. The two foxes snuffled and wolfed down the treats he gave them, then began to chase each other in the snow.

The foxes followed Tikkisi as they would have followed a polar bear, and once he had thought that the pelt of such a fox would make a fine hat, but then the thought of killing one revolted him. No, he could not kill one, for they came to him as messengers of life, full of fun, beautiful to watch, amusingly greedy and catholic of taste.

As the pot came to a boil, the igloo filled with steam, and Tikkisi turned himself to the task of cutting up fish and dropping the chunks into the bubbling water. The delicate flesh would cook rapidly, and at the thought of it, his mouth watered. Steam billowed out of the doorway and was carried down the lake by a gentle breeze, alerting the senses of a big, hungry old bear who had been skirting the edge of the lake. He swung his head and lifted the button-black nose to sniff. Food scents. Out on the lake was an unusual glowing object. He sniffed again. Source of food scents. The bear began to circle the object, curious about it, ignoring the booming and cracking of the lake as it contracted with a drop in air temperature. The booming of the lake, reverberating like a drumskin, disguised the crunch of the bear's paws on the crystalline snow.

Tikkisi dipped his tin mug into the hole and sipped cold water. It was very rare that he drank tea or coffee now, even though he had plenty left. He preferred the taste of water, finding each lake or stream different, and he also liked the rich soup from boiled meat or fish. Now his belly was full, and he lounged against the igloo wall, making jokes to himself that the rumbling and growling of the contracting lake ice was in fact the gurgling of his own belly. Each time the lake made a noise he raised a hand to his mouth and said excuse me, pardon, and giggled to himself. Should he sleep now? No, first he must toss out the mess of fish bones and fragments in the pot and clean the pot with snow. He had enforced tidiness upon himself, partly as a discipline, and partly as a recognition of the need of it if he wanted his equipment to last.

Outside, the foxes waited eagerly, and pounced on the

splash of bones, salty water and fragments of fish flesh. But as they began to eat, the male fox sniffed the air, spun like a dancer, and stared out into the darkness. It was some time before Tikkisi could see the bear approaching, straight and fast, head swinging, his flat feet kicking up little spurts of snow. Tikkisi darted for the sled, pulling the pathetically inadequate .22 from its cover, jacking a shell into the breech. The bear came on, and Tikkisi reasoned it safer to pull his precious little sled away from the igloo, and to get away himself, for the animal would head first to the place that smelled of food. Fifty yards from the igloo he sat down on the sled, holding the little rifle in his lap. There was no point in running, for if he wanted to, the bear could easily run him down.

The bear headed for the narrow entrance of the igloo and enlarged it dramatically with his massive body. He was a good-sized male, ten feet from the tip of his nose to his tail, and he was hungry. The three small fish that remained of Tikkisi's catch went in as many bites. Then the bear burst through the side of the igloo, swiping at a tumbling snow block. The foxes darted out of the bear's way as he rocked from side to side and then slowly ambled toward Tikkisi.

Panic clutched at him, and he thought that it might dominate his actions, for surely Nanook was returning to avenge himself? He was grown now, bigger and more powerful than before, more menacing, invincible. Tikkisi jumped to his feet and fired a shot over the bear's head. The bear stopped. He had not considered the man as a food thing, but was merely curious, and totally unafraid of any living creature. Did this creature threaten? He reared up on his hind legs and Tikkisi was filled with dread and admiration at the bear's huge height.

"Nanook!" he shouted in the language of the Inuit. "Go away! Go away!" And then, in English he yelled, "Go away Nanook, I'm not scared anymore, so go away or I will kill you!"

183

This sudden eruption of sound puzzled the bear, and he stood for a while, rocking and staring, his throat rumbling threateningly. Tikkisi unsheathed his hunting knife, although he did not really think he stood the least chance against the bear with this weapon. The bear dropped to all fours and ambled back to the ruins of the igloo. At this moment he was uninterested in the strange-smelling thing that made noise. Under other circumstances, other times, he might bother to kill it, but not now. He began to lick at the snow where the water from the pot had been tossed, getting the last of the salt taste from it, and then, after a little time, he turned and sauntered with massive dignity across the lake, leaving prints as large as dinner plates.

Tikkisi was trembling. He sat on his sled, hearing the sound of blood surging through his body. He must head back to the safety of his den, and pray that Nanook would not ambush him en route.

It was another two weeks before he saw the bear again. He was out on the sea ice, and had just killed a seal. For three long, silent, cold hours he had waited by a breathing hole, forcing his mind to cancel the cold gnawing at hands and feet, waiting and waiting for the soft sounds of a seal surfacing under the dome of ice and snow that covered the hole. His hunting method was simple and effective. He would choose a hole and wait by it until a seal surfaced, and then he would blast through the ice with both barrels of his shotgun, killing the seal with lead and with the double concussion of the shotgun's twin barrels. He would then snatch up a gaff and secure the seal's body before enlarging the hole and dragging it out onto the ice. A seal represented a fortune in hot, fresh meat, in blubber, and in a dozen different-tasting delicacies of liver, kidneys, heart, brain and all those other special pieces he had come to crave as a child yearned for sweet things.

The bear came across the ice, charged at him and drove him away from the kill even before he had tasted a single morsel, even before he had observed the ritual of giving fresh snow water to the seal. Frustrated and enraged, Tikkisi yelled foul abuse at the bear, but the bear ignored him and tore into the carcass. When Tikkisi came close, the bear roared and faked a charge at him, driving him away. Tikkisi reloaded the shotgun with two rifled slugs, enough to down even this monster. He approached the bear again until he stood within eight yards. The bear growled, but went on feeding. Tikkisi thumbed off the safety catch and aimed the gun at the bear's chest.

"You! Nanook! This is my seal! I killed it! You go away, you thieving bastard, or I'll kill you! You hear me? You hear me?" His voice cracked, and he stepped closer, and the bear rose up on its hind legs, towering above him. He shouted at it again, dirty words, and aimed full square in the middle of the chest. But his fingers locked, and he could not squeeze off the shots, and even as he tried to shoot, other memories crashed at the door of his consciousness. He stood helpless. Had the bear decided to attack him then, he would have been dead. He was unable to use the gun, seeing in the bear another shape, another life. He was furious with himself, impatient for the outcome of this internal struggle, and he backed off, lowering the gun and relinquishing his precious seal to this big male bear, so arrogant and so dominant. The bear ignored him and fed.

Something within denied the use of the shotgun against the bear, yet surely he could not tolerate this banditry, this mockery, this lack of respect? How would the old people have killed Nanook? What about the thousands upon thousands of years that hunters had faced and killed even bigger bears, without guns? He, Tikkisi, must do the same. He must have courage and face Nanook with a spear, and drive the spear into the vulnerable spot in front of the throat the way old Ipeelee had told him.

Back at camp, he began his preparations. He lashed his heavy snow knife to the end of a stout pole. This pole had formerly been one of the uprights to the big tent from the other camp, and he had salvaged it, thinking to use it for a spare harpoon. For hours he sang to himself as he honed the blade, working with file and whetstone on the back of the blade to bring both edges to a point, razor sharp. He tied and untied the lashing several times until he was sure the blade would hold against his most powerful thrust. Then he began to practice outside the tent, driving the blade repeatedly into a snowbank, until the feel and balance of the spear came to fit his arms and hands. The cliff below the burial hill echoed day after day to his exercises. "Yaaaaah! Nanook! I challenge you! Tikkisi will kill you!"

And he thought that surely Nanook had returned to the place of Tikkisi in the deep of winter, believing Tikkisi to be without allies, that he was alone and defenseless. Yes, Nanook came to torment and steal, and perhaps to kill. Tikkisi would face him! And every day he practiced until his body ran with sweat beneath his heavy clothing, and it was in practice, in this daily facing of combat, that fear of combat became lost, or masked.

It was of course inevitable that the bear would find Tikkisi's den. On the first day that Tikkisi discovered the huge prints all about his home, he was seized with momentary panic, but he sat down and dissected his fear, laid it bare, and saw it and mocked it. Part of that fear certainly was that his hiding place, his security, had been found out, but he rationalized that in his present form, Nanook could not inform other enemies of Tikkisi's whereabouts. Tikkisi was not afraid of dying. Yet he did fear that in the face of the bear's power he might again show cowardice as he did once before, in some vague, misty, long-ago battle. Had he been lying to himself all along about that battle? Had he, in fact, lost it?

Now he gave up all but the most essential tasks in order to exercise with the spear, working himself into a cold fury as he remembered the arrogance of the beast as it had driven him away from his seal, out there on the ice. Two weeks passed, and he saw the big, yellow-white animal several times. Once the bear even tried to dig into the snowbanks around the entrance to the cave, but was driven away by Tikkisi's enraged shouts.

Day had begun to lengthen. The land was brilliant, and there were so many ice flowers, delicate branching crystals formed by the freezing of moisture, which evaporated into the desert-dry air from pools of water that came up like moats around the ice-held bergs, and made smooth, green ice lawns, luxuriant with crystal blossoms. In the air, frozen moisture glittered with the brilliance of a million falling diamonds, making golden halos around the sun, and pillars of light all about the horizon.

For the bear, hunting had been poor, and hunger brought him back to the man-thing's territory time and time again, attracted first by the sharp scents of fox urine, and then to the big mound of rock and ice that covered the cache of whale meat. The foxes had been unable to break into this treasure, for each time Tikkisi took food and fuel from it he would re-cement the rocks together with snow and with water from the nearby tide crack. But the bear, with his massive paws, tore aside the rocks as a child might break down a castle of toy blocks. He gorged himself on frozen meat and blubber. When Tikkisi discovered this he was furious, filled with hatred for the bear. The glutton had devoured a month's food in one meal!

187

He rebuilt the cairn with great care, making at the same time a shallow, blind-ended tunnel on one side, into which he froze a hunk of meat and fat. Around the cairn he dangled empty cans, paired on strings so that they would rattle when disturbed. On four sides he rolled large rocks, to which he tied strong loops of rope. Now pleased with his preparations, he looked forward to the bear's next raid.

The bear's second attack on the cairn came on the afternoon of the following day. He inspected the changed surroundings and went first for the chunk of bait frozen into the shallow tunnel. Tikkisi had placed some of the bear's own droppings by the tunnel, so the animal was not too cautious. The rattle of cans merely caused him to snort, and then to swipe at the string and break it, but the sound had been loud enough.

Tikkisi crept from his den carrying the spear, an axe, his harpoon, and line. He loped across the ice to the shore edge where the cairn had been built. The bear's muffled, snuffling grunts were clearly audible as he gnawed and clawed at the meat in the tunnel. Tikkisi approached his enemy from the right side, flexing his fingers around his weapons. The bear heard him and backed out, growling, but then, almost scornfully, went back into the tunnel. His hindquarters looked like the rump of a fat old man in baggy, furry trousers. They looked comical, and showed little hint of the immense strength and speed of which the animal was capable. Tikkisi had realized that he would never be able to face a direct charge, and without dogs, he would have to hamper the animal's movements, and make him rise up on his hind legs. He laid down the spear and axe, taking the harpoon shaft in his right hand, with the stiff, frozen coils of the line in his left. Softly, softly he approached, his eyes on the rump of the bear projecting from the shallow tunnel.

The bear began to back out. With a fierce yell, Tikkisi

dashed forward and hurled the harpoon with all his might. The bear roared and spun around, dislodging the shaft, but leaving the head of the harpoon deep in his flank. Tikkisi dashed around to the opposite side of the cairn and hitched his end of the line through one of the rope loops on the rocks. As the bear charged, Tikkisi prayed that the line would hold, and it did, for although the weight of the rock was nothing to the bear, the tearing agony of the harpoon head ripping sideways into the holding position deep in his flesh caused the big animal to somersault and bite and snarl at the wound. Tikkisi had now snatched up the spear, and was ready for the next charge. This time, the bear jerked the rock over the ground, but the weight and the pain slowed him down, and he turned again, this time to bite through the line, but not before Tikkisi had lunged in and driven the spear point between his ribs.

In agony and rage, the bear turned on the man-thing, raising himself to his full height, towering almost twelve feet. His height was awesome, but gripped with battle fury, Tikkisi jabbed three times into the bear's belly, wounding him badly. The huge animal swung his paws, but actually backed off. Tikkisi advanced, jabbing with the spear, and the bear attempted to drop to his front legs and seize the man-thing in a two-pawed clasp, to bring its head to be bitten and crushed. But Tikkisi stepped inside the grip, thrusting upward, knowing brief despair at the last instance as the shaft of the spear snapped. But the bear's own weight carried the steel blade through the throat and out between the vertebrae of his neck. As death touched his brain, the bear reared backward against the stones of the cache, swiping one last time with his massive paw and ripping the fur of Tikkisi's parka and shirt underneath. Thrashing and gurgling weakly, the bear in his last moments attempted to dislodge the broken shaft which protruded from beneath his chin. Tikkisi ran for the axe and came back with it, leaping up onto the cairn behind the dying bear. The bear heard nothing as the axe came down and split his skull.

The aftereffects of adrenalin in his system caused Tikkisi to shake and tremble, and he knew fearful joy and great sorrow at the same instance. He sat down by the cairn and stared at the bloodied body of the bear, and slowly all fear and hatred drained from him.

"Aiyah! Aiyah!" he whispered. "Aiyah! Aiyah! Nanook is dead. . . . his soul trudges toward the day. . . . Aiyah! Aiyah! . . . The great one is dead. . . ."

And he sat in the snow, rocking to and fro, his head between his hands, sobbing pitifully.

⌁ THIRTEEN ⌁

In a broad fan trace, the twelve dogs kept a steady panting rhythm, marked by the occasional crack of a whip as it flicked under the tail of any dog that seemed about to lighten its bowels in the path of the *komatic* runners. The ice was good, and the dogs strong and well fed. The rich stink of dog farts came back in puffs to Noah and his wife, and as he ran by the *komatic*, Noah sang a poem-chant to himself, sometimes jumping on to rest his legs. Sastrugi, frozen waves of snow, bumped the *komatic* like a boat.

The contours of the inlet were in clear sight now, and in hours they would pass the hill where Noah's great-grandmother was interred. Truly, Kila Umiapik had been a woman of power, and Ipeelee related many tales of her feats. Noah thought it wise to be well past her resting place by nightfall, not because he was afraid, oh, no, for the old woman's spirit was certainly benign. After all, she was an ancestor — but the old, long-ago people demanded much greater manners than the today people, and old women were notoriously unpredictable and easily offended, and he, the foolish hunter Noah, had forgotten much. He reflected as he ran about what would happen in these places in the future, for the young people now were ignorant even of their own ignorance. Noah thought about that a great deal, especially when traveling.

Runners hissing on the snow and ice, dogs panting, things rattling in the grub box as the *komatic* bumped. Travel sounds.

It was Noah's wife who spotted the cairn by the beach, and the strange figure beside it. The figure from a distance seemed to be that of a large man, half sitting and half leaning against the mound of rocks, and it wasn't until they got quite close that they realized it was not a man, but the skinned carcass of a bear.

Noah stopped the dogs on the sea ice and made his way over the tide cracks and up the beach, stopping to yell back at the dogs when they began to yip with impatience. His wife followed — she was quite agile despite her fifty years — and together they stood and stared at the frozen body with dismay.

The bear had been skinned, but the fur of all four feet, complete with claws, was left on, as was the fur of head and neck. It was a strange sight, sitting there like a massively muscled man wearing fur mitts and boots, and a fur bear-mask. It was monstrous. Noah circled it, inspecting the wounds in belly and sides, and the great wound in the neck, and the cleft in the skull which came all the way down to one eye.

"None of these wounds were made with a rifle. Aaieee! Such a strange thing!"

"Hah!" said his wife, "the work of a foolish and lazy hunter!" She prodded the side of the frozen bear with her mittened fist. "See how he has spoiled the skin and taken none of the meat."

"The belly has not been properly opened," observed Noah. How then could the spirit of the bear escape? Could it go through the mouth, or perhaps the anus? Through the split in its skull? Ah, so much he did not know! Noah felt discomfort in this place. He shuffled around and kicked the snow off the beluga skulls. Foxes had been gnawing at them, as they had been gnawing at the frozen, meaty thighs of the bear. "Look! The hunter has taken many beluga!"

Noah's wife dislodged one of the smaller stones in the cairn and peered in. "See here, there is much *muktuk* and meat!"

Noah spoke angrily to her, for it was now clear to him that this unknown hunter was different, and might be easily angered, and it was also clear that whoever he was, he was both fearless and strong.

He walked all around the cairn until he came face to face again with the frozen, naked bear. He paused, looking up at the frosted, bloodied mask, and the split that came to the eye, giving the face a lopsided wink. He caught his breath. Now he understood! It was the white man! The dead one! The Inuit themselves had named him Nanook, and like the great bear, he had been proud of his strength, wishing people to admire and see it, and he too used to make a sign by closing one eye!

And here, squat, naked, massive, the bear Nanook sat winking his axe-closed eye. Noah shuddered and turned away, calling his wife to follow.

All this time, Tikkisi had been watching them from a gully on the other side of the burial hill, and as they headed across the sea ice in the direction of their camp, fully two days' journey away, Tikkisi felt sad and lonely. He had been wrestling with himself as to whether or not he should call to them and invite them to share tea. But he had decided against it, for he wanted to keep his camp a secret for a while yet.

Even at a distance, Tikkisi had sensed their puzzlement as to why the bear had not been butchered, and he practiced to himself the phrases to explain that to him, the flesh of Nanook was taboo. He left the frozen body there as a reminder that he had not feared, that he had won. Let Nanook be gnawed by foxes and pecked at by ravens, let it stay there until summer when it would rot. Let the gulls eat it. Gulls! He glanced up at the sky, imagining for a minute that they flew overhead, staring at him with those satanic eyes. Never would he forget their spying and tormenting, nor how they had tried to enter his mind and make him kill himself. No! Neither had he forgotten that horror on the beach, the eyeless ugliness, with the gulls all around, nagging and squabbling. Well, he had killed them then, torn those white and gray angels of evil out of the sky, hung their bodies to the wind, burnt them, given their guts to ravens, yes, and when they returned from the south he would be waiting for them and ready. Nanook had been vanquished in the season of no gulls, the season when only the ravens and the silent white owl flew, and these birds were his friends. Let the gulls return now, and let them eat Nanook's flesh! Tikkisi was not afraid anymore!

As the future clouded his vision, he caught images of jostling gulls, smell of decay, and other visions too, visions that were blurred over like the images of double-exposed film. Enough.

Although Tikkisi had not taken the meat of the bear, he had taken the pelt, albeit quickly and clumsily, for he did not want the fur to make a rug, but to make a jerkin and pants. Although not too skilled with a needle, he had time and patience, and the end product of his labors was a double-breasted, sleeveless jerkin with a high collar, buttoned with the teeth of beluga, carved in the shapes of seals and whales. He also made bearskin pants similar to ones he had once seen in a picture of Greenlanders. The jerkin left his arms free, but gave his body warmth. With the long fur, over his lighter caribou or fibred clothes, he looked very bulky.

As Noah's *komatik* and dog team became tiny specks in the distance, Tikkisi stood up, lowering the binoculars. As he moved, he disturbed an arctic hare, which lolloped a few steps and then stopped to stare at him.

"Watch out for my fox friends," he said, and then, to himself, "Now is the time to make other friends."

Soon the birds would be returning, and Toodlik would fill the lengthening days with the joy of his cry, and water would run, flowers and grasses grow. Yes, indeed, it was time!

He went back to his den to prepare the little sled for a long haul. He had been out for two days and nights and now the cave smelled stale and cold. He decided to leave right away, taking a few things and a little food, and on the way he would hunt seal. He became eager at the thought of human laughter and company, and was happy at the thought of sharing, of becoming human once more.

Five days after having passed the hill of graves and the meat cache with its strange guardian, Noah's wife was at the edge of the sea ice by their winter huts. She was watching her youngest son trying to drive a team of five dogs. The boy was ten years old, and the dogs knew it, and were having fun with him, stopping and starting and tangling the traces. Although she laughed at the sight of it, her heart was full with mingled joy and sadness, for this was her last male child, and already he was preparing to leave childhood, and soon she would lose him to the company of hunters. Time had passed so quickly since he had waddled around camp on fat little legs, clutching a puppy to his chest. Part of the sadness that was touching her was due to the loss of one son, a fine young man of fourteen, healthy and strong and full of laughter. Who could have thought that such a one would weaken and die so quickly of the coughing sickness? It was one short year ago. One year. Tears sprang to her eyes, and she turned to go back to the warm hut, but something made her stop and look back, shielding her eyes against the glare. She screamed.

Distorted by the ice mirage, the weaving, elongated figure seemed indescribably sinister. As she watched, it changed shape, becoming first squat and short and then immensely long and tall, and it moved toward her son and his little team. The boy too saw the figure and became frightened, and headed the dogs back to camp. Joe ran out, spilling his tea as he came. An old woman followed Joe, and in another hut, Noah woke up and slipped on his sealskin boots and reached for his rifle.

From the door, and squinting with the bright light, Noah followed his wife's pointing finger. He grunted, feeling at once a kind of fear that he had not known for many years, and a satisfaction in that this was something he had foreseen.

"It is that one, Nanook," he said. "He walks like a bear."

"Is it an evil one? Will he kill us?" asked the old woman, who could not see so well herself, but who caught the sudden hysteria that raced from mind to mind.

"It is the one who is a bear and who is a man, who is a man like a bear, and who is a bear walking like a man, who is both dead and alive, and who will perhaps kill us if we have angered him, or if we cannot kill him first."

The old woman shrieked and ran inside. Joe laughed at them. The ice light's dancing tricked their minds. He could see the bear's coat, and that was worth many dollars at the store. He went for his gun.

As Tikkisi neared the cluster of huts by the shore, he could hear the shouting and the noise of dogs, and he experienced a wave of joy. They had seen him, and come out to welcome him! He quickened his pace, leaning against the loaded sled, and beginning to sweat under the heavy bear fur.

He saw the flash of the first shot and felt the numbing shock of the bullet before the sound reached him. Bang! For a second he stood completely still, and then he clutched at his side. The second bullet zipped by just inches from his head. He flung himself down behind the sled and the dead seal lashed to it. They were trying to kill him!

Noah watched the figure go down and claimed the shot.

"No," said Joe, "the shot was mine. Come, bring a knife." The dogs leapt up and down on their tethers, while the boy's team of five dogs strained to chase out across the ice toward the fallen figure.

The old woman stuck her head out of the hut, shouting at them, telling them not to go out to the *angakok* in case it might trick them. She screeched and pointed, for the thing was now up, and moving, and the mirage seemed to create two figures, one standing on the other's head, moving and mixing like a big yellowing hourglass, and with another thing beside it that spread and grew across the ice. It was moving away from them. With a curse, Joe knelt and fired two more shots, but the miraging had become more severe, and tricked him. He ran to his own team, staked out beside his hut and slashed through their lines. His were the best bear dogs on the islands, and it would not get far with his dogs after it. The dogs would track it until they caught up with it, then worry and delay it until the bear tried to fight them, and they would circle it, darting in and biting, dodging its paws until Joe could catch up and shoot the bear dead.

"Quickly, we must take your boy's team and follow my dogs!" Noah looked stonily at Joe and shook his head. "That was foolish," he said gravely. "The bear spirit will make magic on your dogs, and perhaps carry them below the ice, or change them into monsters."

"You speak nonsense! Does the hunter Noah fear the bear because of his wounds? My dogs will corner him, you will see. Let us go!"

"That creature, foolish one, walked like a man. It escaped on two legs and divided its body. A bear becoming a man, having natures of both? This hunter knows that only a shaman or a demon could do that. This hunter Noah will come with you, for he fears nothing, but he will find no bear, and perhaps no dogs. Come!"

Dressed in parkas, and carrying their rifles and knives, they headed out, having first to mollify the women and children, who were all nearly hysterical with terror, and who wailed, saying that it was unfortunate that Neviaksi was away hunting, for he would stay and protect his families, and would not go chasing demons over the ice.

Noah and Joe picked up the tracks six hundred yards out, and Noah grunted as he pointed to them. They were truly man-tracks, big ones, and they were followed by the shallow lines of what appeared to be a sled. Small spots of blood specked the snow.

"Look," said Noah grimly, "it is clear that the pain of the wound has caused him to metamorphose into man form. We must go with caution, for this one will be cunning and powerful."

They followed for two miles, until they came to a high, long, pressure ridge which bisected the bay. On their side of the ridge, Joe's team was snarling and fighting over the carcass of a seal. Noah got off the small sled and walked over, snatching a seal flipper from one dog's jaws, cuffing the dog as it growled at him.

"He has made magic with the dogs, and brought a seal out of the ridge to feed them. They will not follow him. He is in the ice now, perhaps under it in the sea. If we step close to a crack with open water, he may pull us under. Be wary."

Joe stared at the tracks, which disappeared into the tumbled blocks of the pressure ridge, wondering, feeling uneasy now. He had surely seen a bear, or had the dancing of the ice light deceived him? Or was it, as Noah said, magic? Joe no longer believed in magic, or in demons, but he felt uneasy.

"Let us take the dogs and leave," said Noah. "We can ask the old woman to make a song to protect us. Ah, if only Ipee-lee were here!"

"Truly," said Joe eagerly. "You also have the sacred book in your house, and perhaps you can find something within that to protect us, for it also is the book of the white men." Being a pragmatic man, Joe did not believe in spirits or demons, but it was wise to be cautious. They turned the sled around and headed back, having first retrieved the torn seal carcass so that the loose dogs would follow.

In his hiding place, Tikkisi relaxed and lowered the shotgun. To have been forced to kill any of the Inuit was an abominable thought to him, but had they come near him, or tried to shoot him again, then he would have had no choice. He rolled over and lay still, one side numb where the bullet had grazed ribs. Running from them had caused him excruciating pain, but that was all right now, he could control it, and put his mind to controlling the bleeding. But the physical pain was nothing to the shock of having the Inuit try to kill him.

How right he had been to avoid the searching planes and search would begin again, and they would hunt him until they found and killed him. He would have to return to his den, take what he could carry, and hide other things that he would need, preferably hide them in many places. They would never take him!

He sat up, and with a grimace of pain he pulled his little sled out from a leaning block of floe ice. It was a pity to have lost the seal — he felt hunger now. Beneath his clothing, the blood was clotting. It was a shallow wound, painful, but not serious enough to slow him down. He picked his way through the jumble of ice in the ridge and stepped out onto the broad white plain once more. Three dots, far out. Seals. Tikkisi raised his face to the golden orb which had brought out the sea creatures to share its warmth, and he thanked the sun. On the sled was his hunting screen of white cloth, and even with the puny .22, he, Tikkisi, could sneak close enough to a yearling to shoot it behind the ear. Winter and the harshness of the land had taught the young white hermit a patience long forgotten by most of his race. He took the .22 out of its case and loaded it. The shotgun he dismantled and packed away. Then, with the sled harness over one shoulder to keep it away from the wounded side, he headed out over the ice, humming to himself a song to keep his own mind from reaching out to the seals and warning them of his intent.

"I am Tikkisi," he said aloud, "brother of the sea creatures, brother of the loon and the raven."

He did not need the company of humans.

⚞ FOURTEEN ⚟

Three weeks later, at Whaler's Bay, news of what had happened between Joe, Noah and the "bear demon" was brought to the attention of Sergeant Art McFarrow, officer in charge of the district. He listened carefully as Paulasie, his special constable, interpreted what Neviaksi told him. Old Ipeelee had much he wanted to say, but felt that even the sergeant, who had spent many years in the North, would have difficulty in understanding, so he kept quiet and let his younger brother speak. After listening for ten minutes, the sergeant held up one hand, asking Neviaksi to stop. He called through the open door of the office to the constable, another white officer. "Hey, John, get a chair and come in here. You've got to hear this."

The constable came in and they made room for him while the sergeant introduced him to the two hunters. "John, you remember that I told you I had a gut feeling about that British kid that was supposed to have drowned out there on the Beakers? Well, damn it, it looks as if I was right — the kid is still alive."

"No shit? You mean he's been living with the Eskimos all the time?"

"Nope, not that easy. He's hiding. Neviaksi here thinks he's found the kid's hideout." The sergeant turned to Paulasie. "Ask Neviaksi what this hole in the rocks looked like."

With patience, the sergeant got them to fill out the story. It seemed that after the panic at the camp and the abortive attempt to hunt down the man-bear, Neviaksi had returned and insisted that Joe should come with him and try to find what he knew to be the young white man. Neviaksi had been angry, which was rare for him, and he had called the other men names, for he worried lest the white man was seriously wounded and dead or dying out on the ice. Noah had described the meat cache and the dead bear to reinforce his own version of the meaning of the story, and it was to this spot that Neviaksi and Joe had later headed with their dogs. The den was easy to find, and they knew that only Tikkisi could have built it.

"Many things from white man's old camp," said Paulasie, "lots of things, and Eskimo man no steal, Beaker peoples never steal."

"I know that, Paulasie, but get them to tell you a list of the things, and I'll write it all down here. Did they see any other sign, tracks or anything?"

Neviaksi went on to describe the dead bear, killed with a spear, and he related how the young white man had been extraordinarily successful in his hunt, having cached nine beluga and several seals, much fish, and many, many birds. He had been eating well, that one.

"Looks like we've got to throw the book at him for violating game laws," said the constable, half jokingly.

Neviaksi told them then how he and Joe had searched

for miles around, finding well-worn tracks, fishing holes, even snow houses, but no Tikkisi. He had gone, at a guess, just a week before them. Then they had returned, and Neviaksi had made a special trip to inform the RCMP. As soon as Neviaksi finished talking, Ipeelee spoke. The interpreter said something to the old man, then looked at the floor.

"What was that?" asked Sergeant McFarrow. Paulasie looked from the sergeant to the young constable. He did not want to tell them in case they would laugh and hurt the old man's pride, or worse still, make him angry.

"Come on, Paulasie, it's OK, tell us."

"He say that maybe that young white man, that guy Tikkisi is not really alive, but maybe he come back out of the sea, like a spook."

The sergeant glanced sharply at the young officer, warning him with his look not to show any scorn or amusement, but the glance was not needed. The constable leaned forward in his chair, doubly interested now. "Tell us more, Ipeelee."

Now Neviaksi sat silently, allowing his older brother to explain his interpretation of events. The two RCMP officers listened gravely. When the story was finished, the sergeant stood up, hand extended again.

"OK, Ipeelee, and thank you. You too, Neviaksi. Don't worry, we will find the boy, and we won't hurt him. He won't go to jail, have no fear, but he will have to leave the North, go back to his country. Now, let's go over to my house and I'll get my wife to cook us all a big breakfast." He turned to Paulasie. "Take them over and tell Joan, will you? I'll be over in ten minutes or so. See if you can talk them into staying around for a day. Maybe I'll go back with them, you too, and we'll take a look at that cave." As the three Inuit left the room, the sergeant and his junior officer exchanged glances.

"Well, what do you think?" asked the sergeant.

"I think you've got a nice sled patrol ahead of you. Any chance of me coming along?"

"Sorry, John, you'll have to hold the fort. In the meantime, we've got to get a report on this one back to headquarters, and fast. Can you imagine the fun the press is going to have?"

The constable shook his head. "What a story. Hey, you know, you'd better take care going after that kid, he may be crazy. Come to think of it, he probably is crazy. Do you think he killed the other guy?"

"I don't think so, but I'm damn sure they had trouble, and it was the trouble that caused the kid to bolt. Maybe he thinks he's responsible for the death. There may be more to it, and I intend to fit in as many pieces as possible. But there's one thing I know for sure — that kid is going to be hard to find. If Neviaksi couldn't find him, then he's got to be something really special in the bush."

"Yes, sure is hard to believe," said the constable. "Who would have thought a green kid like that could even have survived?"

The sergeant grinned. "Well, you made it," he said. The constable had just completed his first Arctic winter. "Anyway, try to raise headquarters on the radio, tell them briefly what's happened, and tell them we need a plane in a hurry for a search. There's one in Frobisher Bay for sure, and if we can't get that one, maybe they can get us one up from Montreal. I reckon we'll have to find the kid before breakup, which gives up two or three more weeks at the most. If we don't latch onto him by then, we won't get another chance until June."

"Right." The constable stood up and picked up his chair to carry it back to the desk. "I suppose there will be some flack flying around. I mean, the kid has been in the bush, undiscovered, for nine months."

"Yes," the sergeant sighed, "the shit will hit the fan, so we'd better find him this time." He shook his head. "Damn, but this is big country! Down south they never seem to realize how big!"

The prolonged and costly search for Richard Tavett caused more excitement in the southern newspapers than any other air, sea, or land search that had occurred in Canada since the chase of the mad trapper of Rat River, decades ago. Tavett avoided and outwitted his searchers at every turn, covering seemingly impossible distances. Aided by volunteers from the settlement, and by aircraft from the base, the RCMP searched through the months of May, June, July and August, at enormous expense to the Canadian government. Tavett was spotted from the air on three occasions, and on the last time, the aircraft managed to get low enough for the observer to take a dramatic picture of the runaway, face turned toward the aircraft and contorted with anger, with the bow of his kayak knifing waves as he headed through icy rollers at least ten miles off the northern tip of the main island of the Beaker archipelago. That was in late July. The government patrol vessel responded to a radio message from the pilot and headed immediately for the area, but Tavett had disappeared again, probably in drifting pack ice some five miles to the northwest.

The search was intensified, but they came up with nothing. Tavett seemed to be living in the kayak, traveling continually, sleeping and hunting in the drifting ice, coming to shore in remote areas.

Many Northern experts were convinced he really drowned this time, and had not considered that he might actually make the long journey, in rough waters, all the way from the islands to the mainland shores of Hudson Bay. Search patterns missed him by fifty miles or more.

As the months of summer wore on, it became necessary for the government to adopt the official stand that the young Britisher was drowned, or dead of exposure, and finally, in early September, the last search flight was planned. It would fly to all of the outlying Inuit camps, and neither spotters nor pilot believed they would find anything.

⌁ FIFTEEN ⌁

Just as searching aircraft moved in the skies, rumors moved among the Inuit about the one they called Tikkisi. They were aware that he existed, though some knew not in what form — man, ghost, magician, sorcerer, or demon.

"Why else," asked Noah, "would they hunt him so diligently?" The single-engine RCMP Norseman bucked waves and filled the inlet with its noises as it took off, and the two men, who had just been questioned through an interpreter, stood by the shore and watched. Noah looked at Joe, who said nothing.

"Why else?" he repeated.

"Of certainty," said Joe, "the white men do nothing to protect us. They seek him for their own reasons." He sounded scornful, but his mind raced with doubts. Perhaps it was, as many believed, that the white boy was a phantom, a shadow man, and for this reason neither the white men with their planes nor the far-ranging Inuit with their sharp eyes could see him, or if they did, they saw only fleetingly.

"At the settlement, the one they call Ikinilik tells young

men that the presence of the white boy is a disturbance to the *sila* of the land, that he is an evildoer, and must be hunted down by the Inuit so that his soul may be released."

Noah was shocked. He walked away, angry and wordless that Joe should listen to a man like Ikinilik. Unimaginable evil could befall all of them if they knowingly and wilfully murdered the young man. He winced inside at a memory, but that mistake of the spring was a true mistake, and was different. Yet the wounding of the miraging bear figure still troubled him. He directed his feet to Ooniak's tent, trying to put events together in his head. Hunting had been bad. Some days before, he, Noah, had cast a harpoon at a seal and struck hard and fast, yet when the seal dived, the toggle-headed barb had twisted and torn out, and that was something which had not happened to Noah before. Should he perhaps avoid eating seal meat for a month? Or carry a piece of tough square-flipper hide in the kayak? Or something else? He reached the door of the tent, coughed, and went in. Old Ipeelee sat half naked on the sleeping platform.

"They will not find him," said Ipeelee, matter-of-factly, "and neither will foolish Inuit hunters kill him. The land hides him."

"But there is danger?"

"There is danger," said Ipeelee, but he could not tie words to that, for it was a danger whose presence was in past and future, and as he attempted to form it, scraps of archaic words drifted up like larvae in a tundra pond.

On the oil-drum stove that warmed the tent, Ooniak's wife deftly turned a two-inch-thick circle of bannock and moved the thick iron frying pan. Although she did not wish to speak, the words came.

"That one intrudes upon dreams," she said, and Noah sucked breath, and young Annie, who was repairing her father's parka, paled and glanced at Ipeelee, ready to blurt out a protest for a betrayal of trust about her own dreams, but she saw in her grandfather's eyes that he had said nothing. Her mother spoke.

"In a dream, there were many high houses of rock, surrounded by flat pathways of rocks in squares, and above the high rock houses were trees far taller than any we have seen. Trees to the south, where some white bears winter, are not such as these. No, this foolish one saw trees in a dream that did not have pointed tops and leaves like pins, but trees that had leaves as wide as hands, bright green, with fingers like hands, and in the tops of their cloud-snatching branches, many small ravens squabbled, and built nests. Fearful things snarled and rushed about, some higher than two tents, all red, each with dozens of people inside its belly who looked out through the many eyes of the thing. Aiee! Such fearful sights! And there was one man, made of stone, dressed in an anorak, silent and lonely, and looking out with eyes filled with sadness. And there were other people, beyond counting, and voices, many, many voices." She looked defiantly at the two men.

"That dream is no ordinary dream. It comes from another, and not from an Inuit, yet this woman saw it, and others even more terrible." Noah feared the worst, that Tikkisi had been warped by fear and anger into becoming *ilitsitsok* — sorcerer — malevolent, cunning and vengeful, able to dispatch dream demons that entered into enemies and gnawed at their bellies.

Ipeelee shook his head. "Tikkisi is no sorcerer, and no enemy of the Inuit. He does not realize where his dreams fly, even though he is seeking help. Aiee, there was a time when any Inuit child would recognize these things." He sighed. "Tikkisi sends dreams that seek out familiar hearts. Although he partly believes that the Inuit hunt him, his inside does not believe this. All those people who have once bonded to him with some affection, like the traces that secure a running dog to its sled, might be touched. Yet Tikkisi is like the dog, who runs and likes to run, who likes to know the sled is behind, yet who does not wish to stop on smooth ice lest the sled bump into him. Daughter, you gave food to Tikkisi, mended his clothes, treated him as a mother would. Do you really think he would wish to harm you? No, there is no danger for you or for any of us, only for him."

"What danger?" asked Annie.

"Tikkisi leaves his body in dream travels, yet knows nothing of the spells that must be used to protect the body from being harmed while his soul is away. He is changed and changing, becoming closer to the land and to the sea, and this closeness is great strength and great danger. Tikkisi should soon leave, and regain the things of his own origins."

"Can we avert the danger? Help him?" asked Noah.

"When the time comes," said Ipeelee, and with that he closed his eyes, there momentarily catching a glimpse of Tikkisi, resting on an ice pan in thick pack some distance from a shore that was terraced by high, raised beaches more than a hundred fifty feet above the high-tide mark, raised in giant steps around the curve of the shoreline and pocked with the house rings of long-gone ancients. For a moment, a dull knot came to Ipeelee's belly, and the sensation of great clarity of vision that he knew came with the beginnings of starvation. The boy was still strong, but famished. He was, Ipeelee saw, a hundred miles beyond the outer grid of the RCMP search patterns. Ipeelee nodded to himself and opened his eyes. Nothing he had taught the boy would be wasted.

"Ah, but an old man's belly growls for bannock and tea," he said, and young Annie jumped up to fetch him some.

Far off, Tikkisi felt in turn a sense almost of companionship, and he sat up and sniffed, catching in his nostrils strong scents of land. He had not eaten for fifteen days, and those scents made him salivate with sudden memories of bannock, tea, jam, caribou meat, marrow, boiled fish, *muktuk,* and a host of other foods. The ice mass was beginning to circle in a slow, wide wheel and break off at its outer edges, as a headland to the south created currents. He readied his kayak and gear and folded the square of white canvas that had been both shelter and camouflage in his long journey. Overhead, a glaucous gull nagged, but Tikkisi scornfully ignored it. His belly rumbled with each touch of warm land wind, and he began to hurry.

At last it was over, this test of ice, and already it seemed distant. Had he truly flown with the raven and swum with the killer whales, seen himself in layered images, image upon image upon image?

From pan to pan and lead to lead, alternately carrying and paddling, he made his way to the edge of the pack, where a mile or so of open water separated it from land. He had been on moving ice so long that it felt as if the ice were immobile, and the land a floating mass of grays, browns and greens. The kayak knifed toward the shore. There were young eiders everywhere.

Once on land, it took him less than an hour to shoot, gut and skin his first hare, and while it roasted in a covered pit in the shingle, he gathered berries and edible vetch roots from hillsides that were thick with them. A stream ran to the shore, and in it were the remnants of an old stone fishing weir, which could easily be repaired and reused. Ptarmigan cackled in hollows and in slopes, and there were all kinds of shrubs suitable for making tea, or quick, hot fires, and all along the shore were pieces of driftwood, some long enough to make supports for a canvas lean-to, and one fine piece that would make an excellent shaft for a fishing spear. What a good place to regain energy and strength! But what, or where, next?

It might have been from half-remembered descriptions of Ipeelee's father's sojourn in the tundra, or it might have been from curiosity aroused by the inland flight of ravens, or it might have been from a need to reaffirm ties with the land. But whatever it was, Tikkisi determined to journey inland, and find out what it would teach him. He cached his kayak and equipment a mile up the river valley, hiding them well with rocks. He decided to take only his clothes, including a summer amorak to keep off mosquitoes, and a knife, and a hareskin pouch of dried fish and berries. For the first time in all his travels, he went without rifle or shotgun, for something told him that he must not be the cause of any unnatural sounds once out on the wide bosom of the tundra.

Summer was drawing on, and dusk kissed the valleys and slopes for a period of three hours at night, yet these days the butterflies, bumblebees and mosquitoes seemed to be renewed with vigor. At last the time came. Tikkisi, adopted son of the sea, took a long look at its shimmering face and turned his back on it, beginning a journey inward, into the land and into himself.

After ten days of walking he had used all his dried food, and he began to subsist on roots, berries, edible fungi and an occasional small fish caught in shallows. This diet made his body even leaner and harder, and his mind clearer and more gentle. He was no longer a fleeing predator. He walked with his thoughts and songs and allowed his mind to release memories like rising bubbles — memories of Wales, of England, of

Philip, of the months of solitude. However, none of these memories made sense or pattern, for they were isolated, unlinked, and he merely let them pass with the images of sky, tundra, clouds. His mind became a still pond, catching, reflecting.

Winding and turning, the valley cut through cliffs and hills and wide, boggy plains. Most of the time he kept to the ridges, and could see mile upon mile of treeless tundra, freckled with myriad lakes and ponds, desolate, lonely, yet pulsing with the lives of bird, fish, insect, fox, lemming, wolf, and now and then, caribou. He was conscious also of other beings, things which Ipeelee had described to him: demons whose moaning voices mingled with the yips of foxes, and laughing spirits that drank by the banks of streams. After a while, these shadow creatures began to intrude upon the periphery of Tikkisi's vision. Sometimes he would stop walking to listen for them, and let the wind bend around his body, and he yearned to fly, to be totally surrounded by the medium of air. Aiyah! Aiyah! This man's body grows light. His soul shall not be confined by stones! Aiyah! Aiyah! This man's breath is the wind!

He had renewed his former custom of bathing naked in the streams, and sometimes he stopped by a warm, shallow pond to swim. Food was not plentiful, but it was available, and he had learned that it was not the "I" that was hungry, but "Stomach," complaining of emptiness.

As he went farther inland, there were valleys whose ridges were guarded by *inukshuk* — rock-slab figures which for aeons had watched the passing of the caribou herds, channeling some of them to follow a narrowing, blind-ended valley that for the caribou was a trap, and for the Caribou Inuit a place of slaughter and feast. Yet these inland people had long since gone, decimated by starvation and disease. Tikkisi listened to secrets whispered by these stone sentinels as the breezes caught at their slab-edged corners, for indeed there were souls in those figures, dormant *innua* absorbed in part, perhaps, from the hands and hopes and needs of the men who had built them.

For three days, he walked on without sleep or food, going deeper along the valley of the stone men, and going deeper into a trance. Wolves paralleled his course on the opposite ridge, but they were not concerned with him, but with the progress of a single bull caribou down in the valley. The animal was limping from an injured leg, but it was still a big male, strong and wary, and the wolves, fat on lemming and hare, could wait.

Tikkisi walked without feeling the ground, while jaegers dipped at his head, following and swooping until he passed out of their nesting territory. He was both oblivious and acutely aware of them, and of the shallow depressions of their nests, occupied occasionally by downy young, and littered with greenish olive, brown-speckled shell. Startled rock ptarmigan in summer plumage flew off at his approach, and at times he heard the Lapland longspurs, which still thrilled the air with bursts of song as they glided to earth in stiff-winged flight. And all around, the land was beautiful with frost-sculptured rock, the colors and scents of saxifrage and lupine, and the multishaded pastels of tundra lichens, greens, yellows, blue grays.

The valley was drawing to an end, and soon would reach the head of a stream whose arteries were the hanging ribbons of waterfalls. Tikkisi stopped walking and almost fell. In the valley bottom he saw the white of hundreds of bones and antlers, and among the white, he saw the movement of a single bull caribou. As Tikkisi stared and stared, trying to focus his weaving, wavering vision, the bones on the valley floor became a lace of moving, pulsing lines. The single caribou walked a while, then stopped, looking around as if deciding to return. Yet it sensed wolf, and could see the silhouettes of the stone men dominating the ridges around. It stood still among the bones of long-dead ancestors, eyes rolling, ears twitching.

In Tikkisi's sight, the litter of bones meshed even tighter, and began to rise, becoming units, rising one by one, growing fleshed, then covered with swift-grown pelts of gray, silver and brown. There was a forest of antlers down there, moving and moving. Soon the sounds of the waterfalls began to change to the cries of frightened animals, and the yells of men. He saw the men, darting and dodging as their spears were driven between ribs, and the shallows of the stream head ran scarlet. Ah, in the rushing and roaring and hissing and singing there was such a killing going on down there! Tikkisi drew his knife and ran down the scree slope, with one body that flew and another that stumbled. He screamed with exhilaration.

Hearing his voice, the bull caribou began to cross the wide and shallow fan of headwaters, but stopped as three wolves streamed down the opposite slope. Choosing, the caribou faced the approaching man.

He came splashing through the knee-deep water at the caribou, head on, but was in turn driven backward by a powerful thrust of its antlers. He seized them and stumbled as the animal pushed. Tikkisi fell, but hung on, dragging the caribou's head even lower. At this place the water was about two feet deep, and numbingly cold. Tikkisi's head went under water, but he hung on, twisting the antlers. He surfaced again, and saw on the banks the steady stare of three yellow-eyed wolves. It was a stare without malice, but of watchful impatience. It was not an easy fight, and he had to struggle hard to stop the lower points of the antlers from piercing his chest, and all the time he was aware of, yet detached from, the sensations of struggle; the cold of the water, the push of the antlers, the snorting of the caribou's breath, the rolling of its eyes. He thought he saw too the inevitability of death in those eyes, and in that death the passing on of strength to himself and to the wolves. It seemed to be an answer, so simple and complete that it filled him with relief. The knife severed an artery in the caribou's neck and its hooves slipped on rounded stream-bed pebbles. Dying, it fell over and trailed red into the water.

Tikkisi was too weak now to move the carcass, so he gralloched it in the water and let the guts wash out and down in the current. Even then it still took him some time to wrestle the body to shore. The wolves, five of them now, retired to a distance of twenty yards and waited.

The flesh of the caribou brought first strength, and then a heavy torpor. Having flensed the animal, he dragged the hide away from the stream and laid it out over a carpet of thick moss and lichens. He also took away the back muscles and fat, one haunch, and the liver. The rest went to the wolves, who closed in and fed on the ample remains, seemingly oblivious of the sleeping human fifty yards away. As the gentle warmth of afternoon sun dried his anorak and pants on his body, Tikkisi lay snoring, careless of mosquitoes and blackflies, in a sleep untroubled by dreams.

On a rock, at the top of the cliff beside one of the waterfalls, a raven watched.

More than three hundred miles away, old Ipeelee gazed into his mica-flecked rock, heart filled with a happy sadness for a people long gone and for others who would never even know of their passing. Ah, if only the boy had come a generation earlier!

Tikkisi ate the meat as he traveled back toward the coast, going more quickly now, but pausing once in a while to take a fish or berries, or to kill the more stupid ptarmigan with a well-aimed rock. As he came close to where land joined sea, he heard shots, and proceeded with great caution. The shots went on, several at a time, with regular pauses, then several more shots, another pause. Tikkisi crawled to the edge of an outcrop and looked down. His eyes watered, the lids all puffed with mosquito and blackfly bites, narrowed by swelling to slits. At first he could discern only two large ridge tents and a few men. He strained to see, wishing that he had brought the binoculars with him.

White men! Fear jolted his stomach, but soon subsided, for the men were obviously neither looking for him, nor aware of his presence. He came around the outcrop and crept to a lower, closer one. Then he lay for a while watching and chewing on a piece of dried meat.

"Hey, Jack!" shouted one of the men. "Throw one up for me!" The evening air carried the voices clearly, and there was no wind. An empty can sailed into the sky, and three shots from a semiautomatic .22 cracked in the still, violet evening. One shot hit the can. It clattered onto frost-shattered stones and was kicked and bounced by five more shots. Another shout. "Put a rock in the next one, Jack! It'll go further." Another can and more shots. Three men were shooting and one throwing cans, and that went on for twenty minutes until somebody came out from one of the tents, banging on a pot. Laughing and joking, the men went inside.

The camp was in a sheltered bay with a reef well offshore

and fairly deep water inshore. It was not a good place for seals, or for fish. There were no boats on the shore, so the men must have come in by floatplane. Moving very slowly, Tikkisi scanned the land all around, making damn sure no evening stroller would come upon him. Then he waited, the hood of his anorak well up to give some protection from flies. There were things he needed from that camp, before he went around the bay to his own cache site.

After an hour or so, the men came out of the tent again. One went into the second tent. Another took a fishing rod and walked up the shore. Somebody else came out with two buckets and passed within fifty yards of where Tikkisi lay. Two others came out and began throwing things at each other — round, yellow balls which splattered on rocks as the men dodged and ducked and hooted with laughter. Oranges! A taste memory came to Tikkisi and he watched with horror as they threw twenty or more of the fruits around until no whole ones were left. The circling sun dipped down to skim the surface of the sea. Soon the men went in and for a while there was talking and laughing, then quiet.

At two hours past midnight, just before the sun was beginning its climb again, and when red-throated loons javelined out from inshore lakes to feed at sea, Tikkisi took off his anorak lest its rustling betray him, and approached the camp.

It was a warmish night, and the tent flaps were open, and through the mosquito netting at the door of one tent he could see four cots, with four sleeping men in heavy Three Star bags. They must have been uncomfortably warm, for the bags were half open. Kit bags, clothing and rifles lay around the tent, with cameras and binoculars hanging from a nail in the far pole. Tikkisi turned his attention outside, to the boxes that weighted down the tent skirts. Two of them were filled with pieces of rock, wrapped and numbered in small cloth bags. Three more contained tools and canned food. A sixth box held enough .22 and 30.06 ammunition to last a year. Smiling to himself, Tikkisi took one carton of five hundred rounds of .22 bullets, leaving in its place a small carving wrought from caribou antler. It was a carving of a wolf.

From outside the second tent, which was obviously the cook tent, he picked up a piece of smashed orange. It was slightly rotten, but to his taste still sweet and good. Strident snores from inside the tent betrayed the occupant as Inuit. Tikkisi slipped aside the mosquito netting and went inside. Food smells enveloped him.

Menasie Apalialuk, of the Netsilik people, had learned to cook at a DEW-line base on Baffin Island. He was a fine hunter, and once had traveled extensively with his dogs, but now he limped badly from a foot that had been half amputated after severe frostbite. He was a good cook, and a good, solid man who fed his family despite his infirmity. He slept soundly, in a barrage of staccato snores, but his was the sleep of a hunter, aware of the slightest movement. He came awake, thinking the intruder to be one of the young white men, who often sneaked into his tent to steal cookies. But instead he saw a wild looking apparition, with white bear fur around chest and waist, a coppery beard, long hair, deep brown skin, and eyes that were puffed slits in the face. The naked arms were heavy with muscles. Manasie began to reach for his own .303 but the apparition spoke, in the language of the people.

"No. Do not. Tikkisi will not hurt. Sleep. You do not see me, or hear me." The sound of the speech was accented and stilted, almost unhuman, but there was strength in the voice. Manasie lay still and watched as it ate a cold steak, then half a pie, then, smiling, took a can of jam and a loaf of bread before walking out of the door. For a long time Manasie lay still, afraid to move, hearing the calling of female eiders offshore, and the high drone of mosquitoes in the lee of the tent as they blindly probed the weave of the canvas. When eventually he got up and peered out of the tent, the apparition was gone.

At breakfast, none of the white men said anything about the visitor, for none of them had seen him, or noticed the missing food, or the missing carton of bullets, or even the small wolf talisman which Manasie now had wrapped in a piece of sealskin in his pocket. There was then no doubt that the apparition had indeed been a spirit, and invisible, as it had claimed.

Two days later, when Manasie spotted a wolf foraging along the shore, he shuddered, and touched the carving now nestling in his pocket. He felt a mortal dread lest the white men should see the wolf and try to shoot it, thereby angering the *angakok,* who surely was either using the wolf form, or had temporarily invaded the carnivore's body.

But Tikkisi, with his kayak and gear, his new caribou skin and his refreshed supply of ammunition, was long gone. Even so, tales of his ability to metamorphose into animal form or to become invisible would soon be known in every Inuit settlement along the coast. Who could doubt the word of a good man like Manasie Apalialuk?

⌁ SIXTEEN ⌁

It was early October, and the snow was late in coming. Ooniak, Ipeelee, Tommy and their families had moved back to their winter campsite, and they were once again hunting, seals mostly, and especially the bearded, or square-flipper, seals so valuable for the manufacture of boot soles, dog traces, and harpoon lines. The Peterhead chugged along the coast, with Ipeelee up in the bow and Ooniak steering with the long oaken tiller. They swung close into shore, near the mouth of a bay that provided good anchorage, and which had the kind of bottom that favored large shrimps and other benthic delicacies that bearded seal liked to eat. Ooniak watched the small hand and arm movements of his father as he directed them through a channel made difficult by a couple of shoals and several submerged rocks. Suddenly Tommy shouted, pointing excitedly to starboard. It was a pod of killer whales. Ipeelee saw them, and with the seeing, knew other things. He looked from the whales to the mouth of the bay, and observed too that the whales were not hunting, but just loafing around, about a mile from the channel.

"This day we will find him," said Ipeelee. He looked toward the bay, obscured now by mist and by a point of land. "He will be there." Ooniak nodded, for he felt the same things.

"If this be true," said Tommy, "we must take care, and not alarm him. He might try to hide."

They scanned the way ahead, and the echoes of the old engine began to bounce back at them. Tikkisi would hear their engine, and would know it. If he sought to escape, they must let him, but perhaps this time he would not escape. Yes, perhaps Tikkisi would like to talk with an old man who knew many things and who understood much of his struggles.

They anchored the boat two hundred yards offshore in thirty feet of water, water so clear they could see the clouds of silt and sand brought up by the settling anchor. Ooniak launched his kayak over the side, while Tommy and Ipeelee shared another, with Tommy lying inside with his head between Ipeelee's knees. Swift strokes brought Ooniak up alongside Tikkisi, who was paddling his kayak hard, towing in a large, heavy, bearded seal, a male.

Without turning his head to look, and grunting with the effort, Tikkisi spoke the first words he had spoken to them for over one year.

"I see you, Ooniak," he said.

The Inuit grunted and slipped back, deftly hitching another line to Tikkisi's towing line, which was looped through a cut in the seal's lower jaw. Now, with two kayaks, it was much easier. Ipeelee and Tommy had already reached the shore. As soon as the kayaks of Tikkisi and Ooniak touched the beach, Ipeelee and Tommy grabbed the line and began hauling the heavy carcass up the shingle. The other two men pulled their craft up, and then with four of them, the seal slid easily out of the water.

Tikkisi had grown almost two inches taller and probably twenty pounds heavier, with arms and shoulders heavily muscled, and that, with a face tanned almost black from the reflection of sun off water, told of long hours in the kayak. His face had changed, jaw now more square and powerful, beard thicker. He obviously chewed raw meat as the Inuit did. His eyes were steady, and he no longer wished to hear the sound of his own voice. Ipeelee came over and crouched by the dead seal, poking his fingers into the hole where the harpoon had entered.

"The hunter throws well," he said.

"The hunter had a good teacher," the young man answered, his speech grown more stilted now.

"Tikkisi does not seek to hide from us," said Ooniak.

"Two days, we hear the engine," said Tikkisi. "We know it. Yesterday we watched from there." He pointed to a high point by the mouth of the bay. Around his neck were a pair of binoculars, hanging over a necklace of carved beluga teeth. "This man does not believe that Ooniak, his Inuit father, will hurt him. He does not believe that Ipeelee, his teacher, will hurt him, nor Tommy, his friend. It is easy to kill Tikkisi. If you wish to do so, you can do it. The others could not find nor kill Tikkisi. You can. Tikkisi grows tired of running. Now is the time to gather food." He looked at the sky. "Soon will come the long darkness, and ice."

The three Inuit looked at him, and were impressed by the depth and steadiness of eyes that were as blue as the sky, unwavering, unafraid, and old Ipeelee saw that all along he had been right, for these were not the eyes of a crazy man, but the eyes of a man of power.

"The whales are outside," said Ipeelee.

"The sea brothers wait for their share," said Tikkisi, nudging the dead seal with his foot. Tommy sucked in breath. Then it was true — the white man could converse with the big black and white sea beasts!

"The voice of Ooniak's engine travels far under water," said Tikkisi. "It frightens the sea brothers, but I am glad." He looked around the bay, searching in his mind for words. "This place is not good for them." He could not explain. The beaches and bottom of this place might confuse the whales, and maybe it was this knowledge, and not fear of the underwater pulse of the engine, that kept the big bull away.

Tommy fetched a knife and a sharpening steel from Ipeelee's kayak and pointed at the seal. "The hunter wants lines from this one? Boot soles?"

Tikkisi nodded. "We share. For this one, one small line is enough. This hunter has cached more."

The Inuit looked at each other and Ipeelee spoke. "Ooniak and Tommy will skin the seal. An old man desires to talk with his friend Tikkisi. There are many stories, many things to be told, many stories."

Tikkisi nodded and began walking up the beach. He was greatly changed, no longer the talkative and excitable boy he had once been. The old Inuit followed, and they went a long way around the bend of the bay, to where low outcrops of rock poked through shingle beaches, and where grasses and arctic cotton grew. Tikkisi sat down on a flat rock and gazed out to sea. The old man did not know where to begin, and he was having difficulty phrasing his words in the proper manner, because Tikkisi's command of the language of the people was rudimentary. A pity. Anyway, apart from the really important things such as questions of where and how his soul had flown, or of what strange sights he had seen, and what powers he had learned to command, Ipeelee would have to try to persuade the young man to come back to camp with them, and eventually to return to the settlement and have words with the police, who had been seeking him, and who would eventually find him. Ipeelee knew too that the coming winter would be a hard one, because Tikkisi no longer had the equipment and supplies he had had before. He glanced sideways. Tikkisi was motionless, staring out to sea through the entrance of the bay. The old man wanted to ask him about those last days with the one they called Nanook, about his choice of hideout, about the dead bear, and about the dreams that surely had come to him in his solitude. But it was Tikkisi who spoke first.

"I sit with an old one," he said, and Ipeelee laughed, but did not at first comprehend. "I sit with a hunter. There was a time when the sea touched that rock." He pointed to a line of boulders, far up the beach, higher by more than twenty feet than the present high tide marks. Ipeelee's eyes widened with understanding.

"What does the old one say?"

"He wonders about the land of the men who build big ships and who harpoon the great whales. He thinks he would like to travel to see this land, to see many things, but he has fear."

Ipeelee nodded. Long ago, in the time of his grandfather, the whalers had brought their big ships into this bay.

"Look," said Tikkisi, "look there, by your feet."

In the shingle were flakes of flint. Ipeelee picked some up. Long, long ago, the people laid pieces like this in bones, or antlers, or even sticks, and they used them as knives. Long, long ago, when dwarves and giants walked the land, and when the Inuit talked the language of all creatures. Tikkisi dropped to one knee and swept away the shingle, exposing a flint spearhead, two inches long, with a broken tip.

"But the old one thought too much and he broke his spear point. It is not good to think too much. It hurts."

Ipeelee nodded. It was so. A man's mind could make dreams which walk and speak, and if unwary, a man not well versed in the power could create a dream that would take over his body. He took the spearhead and placed it back in the shingle.

"That old one sat here, long, long before the white hunters of the whale," said Ipeelee. "The Inuit have known this land for many lifetimes."

Tikkisi looked back at the present reach of the sea, at the untidy tangles of drying seaweed and driftwood, and the line of ice marks on rocks. Then he looked up the beach, to other, higher beaches, even higher than the one they sat upon, and he looked along the beach, to where the ribs of a long-dead bowhead whale stuck out of mosses. Yes, yes, of course it was so, but he had felt dreams, he truly had, dreams within dreams, and in his dreams time became compressed or stretched, just like an ice mirage, and scenes were shuffled willy nilly so that he saw many futures, many pasts. But he could not interpret. The future and the past happened together, connected, juxtaposed, yet out of phase. He shook his head.

"Many men have sat here to think, as we sit here," said Ipeelee. The old man placed one hand on Tikkisi's shoulder. "Come, let us go back. On the boat we have dried caribou meat and bannock. We have tea and sugar. Let us go to the boat and share it."

The hardened, weather-browned features broke into a smile that had won Tikkisi his nickname among the people. He jumped up and hurled a pebble far out into the water.

"Sugar? Tea? Let us go!"

The old man began to laugh, feeling a wave of relief. It would be over soon. There was no hatred in Tikkisi, and there was no need for questions. With pinions whistling, a flock of eiders skimmed low, low over the water. The two men watched them pass and then started to walk back around the sweep of the shoreline.

The decision was reached without exchanging words — Tikkisi would return with the Inuit to their camp. He felt he could trust these men, that they would do nothing to harm him. The Inuit, on their part, were extremely sensitive to his feelings. The past winter was a matter so crucial, so private, that Inuit hunters would never be so impolite as to broach it first. Should he wish to speak of it, then he would speak of it. However, one thing had to be mentioned.

"Tikkisi . . . the hunters, Joe and Noah . . . they believed that they saw a bear, and they shot at it."

"There are times when Nanook walks like a man," he replied. "I myself have seen this."

Tommy spoke. "A hunter would be sad to hurt a friend."

"When Nanook stands, he is preparing for a fight, and a hunter would try to kill him. This one understands."

The young man fell silent, wishing to say no more. Ooniak went to spin the heavy flywheel and start the engine while Tommy thoughtfully chewed on a piece of dried meat. Tikkisi went up to the bow of the Peterhead to watch for the killer whales. As soon as they were out of the bay, Ooniak stopped the engine so that Tikkisi could show his friends how the big bull answered a whistle, and would come to accept his share of the hunt. After it was done, and the whales gone, Tikkisi stood alone at the bow. In the bearskin jerkin, with his muscular arms bare, he looked like a Norse warrior. Even icy spray caused him no discomfort.

At first fearful, and then solicitous, the women at the camp insisted that they wash and repair the few woolen and cotton clothes that Tikkisi possessed. In truth, his body was clean because of his daily ritual of bathing in cold water. Unblem-ished by the use of chemicals that destroy natural oils, his skin had a sheen to it, and he was really brown, and that, with a manner of walking that was quite unlike that of the settlement white men, made the people feel at ease with him, except, that is, for young Annie, who felt a pull so strong she fought it like a seal against a harpoon line.

Over the period of a week, he became used to human com-pany again, and when they felt him to be ready, the Inuit began to approach the subject of his surrender to the authori-ties. He protested.

"No! I have eaten the creatures and plants of this land, and it gives me shelter and peace. I am no longer a white man, and if I return they will kill me! My flesh has become the flesh of this land. It would be foolish to go to the houses of the men who have been hunting me. Do not make me go!"

Ooniak spoke. "Toodlik, the loon, is the wisest and oldest of all the birds of air and water, and Toodlik returns to the South each year. Tikkisi must also return."

"The police will not permit Tikkisi to live with the Inuit," said Tommy, "even though the Inuit welcome friends. Tikkisi must go."

"Go, Tikkisi, or they will hunt and chase you, and they will always ask questions of the people, and some people will tell them." Ooniak spoke the truth. "Only harm will come if you try to stay, if you continue to hide. No, Tikkisi, that is not good, you must go to the police."

"If I go, they will kill me." He said it simply and with com-plete assurance, and when he said this, the Inuit men looked at each other, and then spoke so quickly that Tikkisi could not understand them. They seemed to argue.

"Tikkisi has nothing to fear," said Ipeelee.

"I killed," said Tikkisi.

228

The old man gazed deep into the young man's eyes and slowly shook his head. "This old man can see into the very back of Tikkisi's eyes, into the dark places that other men cannot see. He sees no evil there. Tikkisi killed, but all hunters kill, and there is no danger or evil in this if the hunter understands what he does and honors the souls of the creatures he kills. This old man can also see that Tikkisi killed a bear, but he sees too that the white man we called 'Bear' died alone. Have no fear, Tikkisi, for you have learned power. Nanook the bear taught you courage, and the whales taught you to share. Listen to the cry of Toodlik — he brings you power — and to the call of the raven also. It is foolish to fear the settlement. Go, and one day you will return to us, and never leave. If you do not go, then you will leave and never return."

"We will go with you to the settlement," said Ooniak gently, "and we will speak to the police and tell them that the Inuit regard you highly, as a friend and a brother. They will not hurt you."

Tikkisi hung his head, stared at a spot on the grubby old Grenfell cover of Ipeelee's duffel parka. Then he looked up.

"Does he who faced Nanook with a spear fear the weaklings of the settlement?" said the old man softly. Old Annie, who had listened to the talking, pushed through the circle of men and crouched down beside Tikkisi, laying a wrinkled hand on his forearm.

"The birds of summer always go, and they always come back to the land of the people," she said. He looked at the old lady, and then over her shoulder to young Annie, and in the young girl's eyes there was something that tugged at his chest.

"Tikkisi will go," he said, and they all sighed and began to laugh, relieved that it was over and that the right decision had been made — for had it not been made, the council of hunters would perhaps have been forced to restrain the young man physically, and the thought of that was repugnant to them. It was good now.

There was nothing Tikkisi could have done to oppose that decision, for it seemed not to have been made of his personal volition, but rather as if his life forces had been agitated and drawn with the life forces of buntings, longspurs, eiders, king eiders, old-squaws, mergansers, hawks, loons, and all the other south-goers; drawn too by the porpoising herds of harp seals, and by the whales that began to move to ever-open waters. Tikkisi was drawn with all of this, and he, like them, felt a need to complete things.

Months of solitude, and of concentration on the process of living, had brought him to realize that the walls within his mind prevented him from being a proper, whole man. These walls had served their purpose, allowed him to gain strength, but now he was steady and tranquil enough to begin the terrible work of tearing them down. To do this he must go south. Many secrets lay south.

Tikkisi, in the present, remembered the one who had been Tik, in the past, and he knew that Tik's origins were in one called Richard Tavett, although Tikkisi could not really recall what Richard Tavett had been like. He had to know Richard Tavett, he had to make the snake eat its tail. He sat quietly, thinking, and young Annie could not keep her eyes away from him.

The women made tea, while the men fetched in meat to boil, and Ipeelee brought his hand drum and made a song. Old Annie sat huddled under a blanket by the oil-drum stove, watching the two young people, seeing visions, wondering if she should tell the white hunter the various paths of possibilities she saw in his future. Autumn frost came down with hastening nightfall on the outer canvas of the double-walled tent.

The fo'c'sle of the Peterhead was tiny, and they were all jammed together, Tikkisi, Ipeelee, Tommy, young Annie, Tommy's wife, and three dogs that Ooniak intended to give to a cousin at Whaler's Bay. Inside it was warm with the smells of dogs and humans, of tangy seal skins, and with the softer scents of the thick caribou skins laid over the plywood decking. Only Ooniak was outside, his parka cover dark with dampness and the fur trim bedraggled with a misty drizzle, through which he steered by feel, knowing the push and pull of currents around the shoals that stood off the mouth of the big river.

Soon the settlement appeared through the mist, gradually taking form, tinged gray and mud brown at first, and then came the red roofs and white walls of the Hudson Bay Company post and the flag hanging limply from its tall, whitewashed pole. Above the eroded sandbanks on the settlement side of the river, a few dogs howled miserably in their chained lines. Gray-bottomed freighter canoes lay along the shore, and here and there were kayak stands, sad frames among the mess of rusting oil drums. Oil drums — thousands of them! Tikkisi heard the dogs, and recognized the different feel of the boat as it headed into river water, but he did not wish to go up on deck and look.

At the dock, where a few barges were moored, old oil drums and a wrecked truck stood out against the wet yellow of the sandbanks. There was a chill, a scent of snow in the air, and inland, brooding clouds gathered. God, he thought, this is an ugly place. He wished he were back on the islands, and Annie seemed to pick up his thoughts, and she smiled, and touched his arm, trying to reassure him. Ipeelee began to gather together Tikkisi's things while Ooniak brought the boat into the dock. A dog in the cabin yawned, and another humphed in seeming annoyance at being disturbed. Tikkisi gazed into An-

nic's eyes and wanted to kiss her, but didn't, and Annie saw
this and loved him, but said nothing. Then he went up into
the drizzle and the gray, wishing many things.

"We will take your kayak and tent, your harpoon, gaff,
guns, pots and fishing nets to the house of the missionary, for
he is a good man and will keep them safe until you return."

"No," said Tikkisi, smiling at Ooniak sadly. "This one
would prefer that his Inuit father and brothers keep and use
these small things, and remember a man who was long lost,
and who found meat and warmth and laughter."

"Aiee! It is much!" said Ooniak, who greatly admired the
German kayak, and the fine English shotgun.

"It was of use to a hunter and a traveler, but to a white man
who must leave, it is a poor and sad gift; it is nothing. The
loon goes south with nothing, but Tikkisi will take this." He
picked up a packsack containing a few clothes, a sleeping bag
and a dozen small carvings he had made from the teeth of the
beluga. His chest was tight with emotion, but he allowed nothing to show in his tanned features, and likewise Ooniak felt
a similar depth of emotion but showed nothing. Ooniak took
Tikkisi's hand and shook it many times.

"Come, let us go."

The native people at the settlement wondered at first who
this white man could be, for he was dressed so unusually in
patched woolen trousers, a thick shirt cut away at the sleeves,
and a jerkin of white bear fur. No word of a stranger had
come in from the hunting camps — had he traveled far? They
exchanged nods and smiles and greetings with him, and some
shook his hand while Ooniak and Tommy checked the moor-
ing lines of their boat. A few guessed the truth, but would not
ask directly.

Together with his friends, Tikkisi headed up toward the

RCMP post, feeling so strange and out of place, feeling as if he were walking without touching the ground. Yet he was unafraid. A small crowd of natives followed to see what would happen. Curious indeed was this tall, muscular, brown-faced stranger who seemed at the same time both different and similar.

⟿ SEVENTEEN ⟿

Sergeant McFarrow glanced out the window and saw the group approaching. He recognized the three hunters immediately, but was momentarily puzzled by the central figure. Good heavens, he thought, it's a white man. A stranger. What the hell had he been doing, and where? And wasn't that a polar-bear skin he was wearing? Then the sergeant knew. He shouted.

"John! Hey, John! Get your butt in here, quick!" The constable left his desk and came into the office. "What's up?"

"Do you see what I see? It's that limey kid – the Eskimos have brought him back!"

The two white officers and their Inuit special constable waited in the office for their visitors to come in. Outside, a small crowd waited.

"Richard Tavett?"

It was an echo from the past, distant, unreal. The room expanded and shrank and seemed unbearably hot, and under his tan, Tikkisi blanched. The sergeant had his right hand extended, and his eyes were questioning, but not unkind. Tikkisi looked at him, unblinkingly, and tried to adjust his perception.

"Well, you are Richard Tavett, aren't you?"

Tikkisi took the hand and nodded. If he was to be Richard Tavett, then so it would be, another metamorphosis was not impossible, and was probably the only way to adjust to things in this world. Very well, he would become this double-named being who was one with the South people. Stiffly, he answered. "Yes, I am Richard Tavett."

The sergeant let out a long sigh. "Jesus, where the heck have you been and what the heck do you think you've been doing all this time?" Tikkisi, Richard Tavett, looked away, searching for the comforting presence of his Inuit friends, but feeling them now grown distant from him. The questions that this man asked . . . they were wrong, impolite, improper. He tried to answer but found himself stuttering badly, unable to form the English words. Ooniak answered for him. Paulasie interpreted.

"Eskimo man Ooniak say this guy been looking for something for a long time, and he don't want people to stop him looking." Then, following with his own thoughts, he added, "Maybe this guy was looking for the other man?"

"Well, sit down," said the sergeant. "I've got some writing to do."

The local armed forces base commander was informed, and so was the RCMP's G Division headquarters. Within hours, cabled orders came from division headquarters to hold Tavett in custody and to send him out on the first plane. The minister himself insisted that deportation proceedings be initiated immediately. Of this, Tikkisi, for that was who he really was, knew nothing.

It was on the local airbase at Whaler's Bay that Tikkisi got his medical. When it was over, the doctor drove him and the constable back to the RCMP post, and went in to talk with the sergeant. John, the constable, then took Tikkisi for a meal and to try to find him some clothes more suitable for civilization.

The doctor laid a manila file on the sergeant's desk. "Art," he said, "I've got the results of the medical here, and I want to talk to you about it. I think it's significant."

"Take a seat, Doc, and tell me what shape he's in." The doctor sat down and took out his pipe.

"Physically, he's in really amazing shape. Truly amazing. He weighs one hundred and eighty-eight pounds of mostly muscle. Everything about him is good, eyes, teeth, the lot. I really did a thorough examination. However, there's one long scar on his chest, and although he refused to talk about it, I think it's a bullet graze, about six inches long and probably went deep enough to touch a couple of ribs. Nothing serious, but close, really close."

"A couple of Eskimos out on the Beakers thought he was a bear or a devil and took a potshot at him. He's lucky they missed."

"Lucky indeed. Anyway, to continue about the physical I gave him, his heart rate is unusual. It's in the middle fifties at rest, which is about equivalent to a good long distance runner, and indicative of the shape he's in, but what got me was that while I was taking his pulse he started to fool around with it. Art, I'm not kidding you, and I nearly didn't put it into the report because I might get accused of drinking on the job . . . but the guy can alter his pulse rate. It's phenomenal. In less than five minutes he put it down to twenty a minute, and then brought it straight up to eighty, and just sat there, smiling at me."

"How could he do that?"

"Beats me. I've read about Indian yogis doing it — you know, mind over matter."

"Seals," said Sergeant McFarrow.

"Come again?"

"Seals. Whales too. They put their heart rate down when they dive. The guy has been living with them so long he's turning into one." He laughed, then wondered what had made him make a joke like that.

"Well anyway," continued the doctor, "he's fit and has amazing control over his body, but there is something else, Art, something which I think is very important. There's a very nasty scar on his head, right on top. I ran a couple of X rays on the skull, just to see, and sure enough, there it was. That stuttering of his made me suspect it. Look at this."

He opened the file and held up a couple of large negatives.

"See that tiny line? That's a healed fracture. He's very lucky to be alive. However, look at this, too, see it? On the cheekbone, left side. No mistake about that. At some time he took a hefty clout in the face, and it broke his cheekbone."

The sergeant stared at the negative. "Yes, I see it. Doesn't show on his face now, does it? Do you think that this could have been caused by a fist?"

"Indeed, a right fist. I've seen this kind of fracture before. Mind you, the man who delivered that blow had to be powerful, and probably big too. I wouldn't want to try slugging Tavett myself, not in the shape he's in."

"Yes, it's fitting together, the whole picture. Do you know anything about the guy he was with? The other Englishman? He was a big man, six foot four, and a build to match. I'd guess they had a fight out there."

"That's your department, not mine," said the doctor, "but what is crucial is that the guy has amnesia. I don't just mean amnesia for the period of the accident, but a more severe loss of memory. He doesn't seem to remember the place he was born, his family, school, anything. It's going to be tough for him, going out of here."

"Are you sure about this amnesia?"

"I'm not a psychiatrist, so I can't be sure, but with that scar and the crack on his head, which certainly went along with a severe concussion, and then with his stutter and his eccentric behavior for the past year and more, my bet is that the guy is not faking. Handle him carefully Art, because he's going to be submitted to a hell of a lot of pressure, and he could go off the deep end."

"You know," said the police officer, "a loss of memory explains it, and maybe it will make those buzzards down south go easy on the kid. Did I tell you that I've got orders to keep him under arrest?"

"You're not going to lock him up, are you?"

"I don't want to, but my orders tell me I should. He's caused a lot of trouble, but personally I can't help feeling admiration for him, and if he's gone through a cracked skull, a beating, being shot at, and has survived on the land so long, then he must have something going for him. Right now he's sleeping in our lockup, because when he came in we had no other place for him, but if he runs again then my neck will be on the block. There's only two of us here, so we can't sit up and guard him. I'm afraid I'm going to have to lock him in the cell, just overnight. In the day he's free to wander around because John or I will keep an eye on him."

"Well," said the doctor, "I said I was no psychiatrist, but I don't think that jailing the guy is the right thing to do. He came in by himself, and if he's treated right, he won't run away."

"Yes, I know. We'll try to make it look good for him, and we won't treat him as a prisoner, but I can't help it at night.

238

God knows how they'll treat him when he gets out, though, because a lot of big people are mad at him. But I appreciate the information, and the advice, and I'll see it gets to the right people."

He went over and plugged in the electric coffee pot. "Not much of this has leaked out to the press yet, and we should be able to get him back to UK or to a hospital or somewhere without too much fuss. But tell me, do you think he is at all . . . well . . ." he touched his temple with his forefinger.

"I don't think so. Not mad crazy anyway. Strange, perhaps, but not dangerous. Actually he has admirable composure, very relaxed, reflective."

The sergeant stood and fetched cups. "Good. Well, how about some coffee?"

"Sure," said the doctor, putting the X rays back into the file.

It was still dark outside when Tikkisi realized he was locked in. With this realization came recognition of his situation. He saw where he was: locked in a cell like a criminal. Through the grill in the heavy door, he peered at the office, saw it as a cramped space, full of unpleasant and unnatural corners, edges, angles and straight lines. Angry now, he slammed his fist into the door.

"No!" he raged. "You didn't capture me, I came in on my own accord, of my own free will. You have no right to put me in a cage!" But only the steady throb of the settlement generators answered him.

At seven-thirty, Sergeant McFarrow hurried over from his house carrying a pot of freshly brewed coffee and two clean cups. His wife had invited Tavett to have breakfast with them, but first he wanted to try to explain to the young Britisher the situation he was in vis-à-vis Canadian immigration laws. He fumbled with the double latch on the outer door and got into the office. As he poured coffee for them both he called out in a cheerful voice to tell his prisoner that he would have him out in seconds.

As he opened the door he saw Tikkisi standing there, but never expected the sudden lunge. With a mighty push, Tikkisi sent the sergeant reeling against a filing cabinet, banging his head against the metal edge. Stunned, and bleeding from a superficial cut, the sergeant fell to the linoleum floor. Tikkisi was shocked at what he had done, for he had not meant violence to the police officer, he had only meant to push him out of the way and get out of that hateful box. Now he stared at the fallen man, and at the bright red trickle from his head, down one cheek, and onto the uniform shirt. Tikkisi almost fainted. Blood. Red blood. Hell is a vortex, black and red, and he was being sucked into it. He had to get away, to get away from the nightmare visions that began pushing into the edges of his consciousness. With an awful scream, he rushed for the office door.

Bill Jacks, the Northern Service officer and general administrator for the settlement of Whaler's Bay, was walking over from his house to the RCMP office. He was carrying his rifle, and was going to tell Sergeant McFarrow of his intention to go over to the dump and shoot some stray dogs. These dogs, half-starved and vicious huskies were a typical nuisance at many northern settlements where the natives no longer used the animals enough, and no longer wished to feed or care for them. In some settlements, children and even adults had been mauled or killed by the stray packs, and the night before, Bill Jacks's own daughter had been badly scared by them.

As he neared the office he heard a scream from within, and without thinking, he levered a shell into his 30.30 Winchester. In rushing to the door, Tikkisi had not realized that it had a double latch, and so he rattled the old handle violently, found it unyielding, and saw it as another barrier to his freedom. In mingled panic and rage, he tore the black and red fire axe from the office wall.

Bill Jacks opened the door and stood there, seeing the sergeant, his good friend, lying by the opened door of the cell, with head and chest bloodied. He saw too a wild looking young man, eyes full of anger, seemingly berserk, standing there in his fur jerkin and grasping the heavy fire axe in his hands, with brawny arms rippling with muscle. The apparition reminded Jacks of a Viking warrior. He raised the rifle.

"Take it easy, man, and put that axe down. You can't get away."

"I can, and will," hissed Tikkisi, stepping forward.

Bill Jacks fired.

As the sergeant was trying to clear the fog from his vision, he heard the bang and saw the exiting bullet blow a ragged hole out of the young man's back and bury itself in the wall above him. Tikkisi staggered, but did not fall. His body was so pumped full of adrenalin that he felt only the force of the bullet passing through him, but no pain. With the axe held straight out in front of him he roared and charged, hurtling Jacks backward through the doorway and out off the step and onto the ground. He then threw the axe down and snatched up the rifle. He whispered, and it was an awful sound, for the double wounds in his chest sucked air in unison.

"I don't want to kill any of you," he said tightly, "so don't come after me." And then he walked away.

Limping from a badly wrenched ankle, and holding a handkerchief to the cut on his head, McFarrow reached the doorway. Bill Jacks got up.

"You OK, Art?" he said.

The veteran police officer merely stared at him, and then whispered what sounded like a prayer.

"Where did the kid go?" Jacks pointed toward the river. Having heard the shot, the corporal came running from his quarters, pistol in hand.

"Put that damned thing away, John," said the sergeant. "Get a vehicle, a stretcher and a first-aid kit. Don't worry about me, it's nothing. You, Bill, get the doctor down here fast, and then make sure that nobody, I mean nobody, goes near that kid." Wincing more with chagrin than pain, he dabbed at the cut on his head.

"Oh Bill, Bill, why the hell did you shoot him? He just wanted to get out."

"I thought he . . . well, he was standing there with that axe, and you were on the floor, so . . ."

"So you blew a hole in his chest with a hunting bullet! Oh Christ!"

White-faced and trembling now, Bill Jacks said no more. He had acted instinctively. It was an accident, but he would never be able to forget the way the young man had looked at him.

Over the water a slight mist softened the shapes and colors of ramshackle Cree and Inuit houses that were strung along the banks of the widening river. Knowing that running would only hasten the loss of blood, Tikkisi walked, with one part of his mind centered on the wounds, seeing them whole and unhurting and isolating them from the uninjured parts of his body which he encouraged to function slowly, quietly. He knew he was going to die, but he wanted first to reach the water. Groups of Cree and Inuit came from their houses and Tikkisi felt a momentary panic that hurtled him into pain and made him stagger and cough blood. Would they try to stop him? But even as this thought and the accompanying agony surfaced, peace touched him and he saw the people as if at the edges of a gray-edged tunnel.

To Ooniak, who had heard the shot and who had known immediately whence it had come, the sight of Tikkisi approaching them only compounded the horror. At first he had thought that Tikkisi had killed a Mountie, for all of the people knew now that they had locked him in their little room. But now, seeing the terrible patches of red staining the white fur, he was reminded of a caribou he had once seen shot this way, walking steadfastly and clinging to life far longer than anybody could have expected. Ooniak had shot the animal again, killing her, and then, on opening her belly, had found a calf within hours of being born. The female caribou had clung to life with the same intensity that Tikkisi now showed, but what was it that he had to do? And why had the white men done this to him?

"Father," he cried in anguish, "we must help him!" But at that moment Ooniak was not thinking of the mortally wounded young man, but of the grief that this would cause his daughter.

"He will be helped," said Ipeelee, and all the people around, even those who had no faith in the shaman's power, felt him reach out and put a barrier around the wounded man, so that none could touch him. Walking calmly and resolutely toward the shore, Tikkisi approached, and the people stepped quietly aside. A Cree elder looked questioningly at the old Inuit, and as if answering his thoughts, Ipeelee spoke in stilted Cree.

"In a dream we have seen this," he said, and the elder nodded.

"Our people will not interfere."

"Is this white man not wanted by the police?" asked a young Cree, holding a rifle.

"We know this man and he is good," said Ipeelee, "but he

has made himself a part of our land, and it could not be. The white men do not want him, for he came to them and it is they who kill him. We have seen dreams, and we know that great evil will come to all of us if we allow them to bury him under the dirt."

The young man with the rifle stepped aside and Tikkisi passed.

Tikkisi tried to lift a sealskin kayak from its frame, but it was too much and he staggered, smearing blood against the poles of the frame and speckling the sand around his feet. With tears running down the cheeks of an otherwise impassive face, Ooniak reached up and lifted down the kayak. Critically, he examined it, seeing the seams all dried and shrunken. He glanced at his father.

"That is the kayak seen in the dream," said Ipeelee. It had belonged to a hunter, gone south to Montreal with the coughing sickness. It had not been used for two years, yet the smell of seal still clung to the dried skin. They carried the kayak down to the water and left it for Tikkisi to climb into. Nobody touched him, but Ipeelee handed him a paddle. Ooniak, and indeed, several others, felt that perhaps they should seize Tikkisi and carry him to the hospital, but the will of Ipeelee held them all immobile and speechless, incapable of doing anything but watch as Tikkisi pushed off from the bank. Caught in the current, the kayak swung around so that he faced them. His face was pallid, his mouth flecked with blood, but his eyes were afire with life.

"This one sees you Ipeelee, and you Ooniak," he said. Then he dipped one blade of the kayak and swung away from them all.

The pickup truck tore along the track, and the sergeant grimaced as his ankle was jolted by the bumps. It was tightly bound with an elastic bandage, but he still couldn't walk on it. In the back of the truck, Paulasie hung onto the stretcher and the first-aid kit.

"I should think he would head for the Eskimo camp," said the corporal, and his superior nodded. When they reached the camp they stopped the truck and wound down the windows. Nobody came out to see them, there was no shouting, no dogs barking.

"It's too quiet. With a man hit that bad, somebody would have noticed, and there'd be a hell of a racket going on. Let's go. He can't get far."

Out of sight below the high sandbanks of the shore of the river, the small and silent crowd watched Tikkisi leave. As they drove away, Sergeant McFarrow suppressed a nagging feeling that they were being pushed away, urged to go by something – perhaps by the quiet censure of the native dwellings. They headed back along the track that connected Cree and Inuit villages to the more orderly and uniform dwellings of government personnel. Even though they passed it, none of them saw the rifle dropped on the track and the trail of blood spots soaking into the sandy dust.

The effort of paddling caused him such intense pain that Tikkisi had to fight hard to separate himself from it and to cling to consciousness. The tunnel of grayness was darkening and beginning to constrict, and he spoke out loud to muscles and limbs, willing them to work against the awful fatigue and heaviness. The kayak, helped by the river, went swiftly out to the sea.

Around his legs and buttocks there was a coldness, and he realized that the kayak was filling with water, and becoming heavier, heavier, slower, yet still he paddled as sunlight, dappled and pearly gray, glinted through broken altocumulus. He wanted to sing now, but could not, yet even as he wrestled with this problem he heard voices singing within him, many voices, some of which he recognized. The kayak was almost full of water now, and when he looked down he saw water around his waist, stained brilliant red. The red color was inches from the top of the cockpit. He stopped paddling and dipped a hand over the side, tasting water that was rich with the salty taste of the sea. How far had he come? He looked back, but there was nothing now, no settlement, no shore, no people, it was all gone and there was nothing but sky and sea and the spreading redness spilling slowly over the wooden rim of the cockpit. Then a raven flew over, calling with a note like a bell, and Tikkisi looked up, seeing the black raven wings growing and spreading over the sky, covering it with darkness. For one last time he looked through his own eyes at his hands, and then he was gone.

The people on the shore, Inuit and Cree alike, gasped with fear and wonder. They saw him paddle out in the kayak, and now they could see the young man, less than half a mile out, sitting upright in the water. The sinking kayak was no longer visible, its top deck was awash, and to the people who watched, it no longer existed. Only the man, sitting upright in the sea, was reality. Silently, they watched as he slowly sank from view.

Through the eyes of the circling raven, Ipeelee looked down and called to him . . . Boy-who-smiles . . . come . . . come . . . and he heard, and went, and Ipeelee was no longer there in the raven, but was back on the shore with the rest of them, and it was Tikkisi who looked down, seeing the red patch around the sinking body, and seeing too that Annie had run to the headland, eyes frantic with grief.

"It's all right, Annie," he called to her, but she couldn't hear him for she was looking in the wrong place, looking out where the body he had been using disappeared beneath a gentle swell.

A wail began to rise up from deep in her body, a loon cry, surfacing through the depths of what had been patience and quiet belief, for she could not see, so she choked down on the cry with an emotion that was almost rage, and then she clawed at the little leather pouch with the loon carving that had hung for so many months around her neck. She broke the string, gripped the pouch hard, feeling the warmth in it, then she threw it, together with her dreams, far out into the water.

It was peaceful now, and the great spreading black wings of the raven became first translucent and then brilliant with colors. Ipeelee turned away from the crowd and walked away, his eyes wet with tears and with mingled joy and sadness in his old, old heart. He knew; in truth he had always known.

And they never found the body of Richard Tavett.

꒦

Aiyah! Aiyah!
This man's name will be remembered.
Aiyah! Aiyah!
This man's name will be remembered.
Aiyah! Aiyah!
This man's spirit
Will not be contained by stones.
Aiyah! Aiyah!
With the wind it will be blown
Among the grave mounds
And by the marker cairns
And across the bay

To the place where the gray
Of water-sky
Dips to the offshore lead.
Aiyah! Aiyah!
This man's spirit
Will see the ringed seal,
Taste his liver and heart,
The sweetness of his warmth
And the joy of past hunting times.
Aiyah! Aiyah!
And on the point, from the camp
Comes the cry
Of a baby.
Aiyah! Aiyah!
This man's spirit will fly
Toward the crying
And enter through the mouth.
Aiyah! Aiyah! Aiyah!
This man's name will be remembered!
Aiyah! Aiyah!

— Old Ipeelee's father's song.
Hudson Bay. Date unknown.